THEATRE SYMPOSIUM
A PUBLICATION OF THE SOUTHEASTERN THEATRE CONFERENCE

Representations of Gender

on the Nineteenth-Century American Stage

Volume 10

Published by the

Southeastern Theatre Conference and

The University of Alabama Press

THEATRE SYMPOSIUM is published annually by the Southeastern Theatre Conference, Inc. (SETC), and by The University of Alabama Press. SETC nonstudent members receive the journal as a part of their membership under rules determined by SETC. For information on membership write to SETC, P.O. Box 9868, Greensboro, NC 27429-0868. All other inquiries regarding subscriptions, circulation, purchase of individual copies, and requests to reprint materials should be addressed to The University of Alabama Press, Box 870380, Tuscaloosa, AL 35487-0380.

THEATRE SYMPOSIUM publishes works of scholarship resulting from a single-topic meeting held on a southeastern university campus each spring. A call for papers to be presented at that meeting is widely publicized each autumn for the following spring. Authors are therefore not encouraged to send unsolicited manuscripts directly to the editor. Information about the next symposium is available from the editor, Susan Kattwinkel, College of Charleston.

THEATRE SYMPOSIUM
A PUBLICATION OF THE SOUTHEASTERN THEATRE CONFERENCE

Volume 10   *Contents*   **2002**

4   CONTENTS

Introduction

THE ESSAYS IN THIS VOLUME of *Theatre Symposium* were selected from among papers delivered at the April 2001 SETC Theatre Symposium, "Representations of Gender on the Nineteenth-Century American Stage." Randolph-Macon Woman's College in Lynchburg, Virginia, provided a perfect setting, particularly given that the college had recently acquired a number of items owned by Charlotte Cushman, including the great actress's writing desk. The spirit of Cushman seemed quite present during the two days of dialogue among several dozen participants, as she was invoked in many presentations, and her famous cross-gender performances and place in nineteenth-century American culture were referenced in the keynote speeches of Susan Cole, Lisa Merrill, and Elizabeth Reitz Mullenix.

In my opening remarks I observed that although both the masculine and feminine were categories guarded and contested throughout the century, it was the image of "woman," and what constituted the sanctioned performance of that social role, that dominated much of Victorian culture. There were expectations of the actress in particular, even as a "public" woman, to conform to a kind of "moral performance" because of the mere *fact* of her gender. The ideal expounded by the Cult of True Womanhood was one rarely conformed to yet one that influenced the late twentieth century's study of nineteenth-century culture. The senior, midcareer, and emerging scholars addressed the issues and icons contained in little-known scripts and familiar melodramas and examined the intersection of the on- and offstage lives of both overlooked and popular performers, in both legitimate and illegitimate venues.

The conference, a productive intersecting of theatre history, literary theory, and cultural studies, explored such questions as, What was the perception of appropriate gender roles, both on and off the stage? What constituted gender transgression in cross-dressed performances, in adult roles played by children, and in parts played by older women? Is it possible to discover the real person, regardless of gender, beyond the layers of performance that a nineteenth-century actor assumed? How did the relations of the genders literally play out, both in the scripts and in the enactment of melodrama? How did particular female performers embody the nineteenth-century notion of the "true woman"? What, in turn, signaled "manliness" in the theatre?

The essays by Laurie Wolf, Karl Kippola, Brian Carney, and Dorothy Holland offer different perspectives on the performance of both masculine and feminine gender. These authors look at how gender relations were negotiated in both the scripts and stagings in popular melodramatic scripts and entertainments. The use of stage space by characters—the gendering of the literal territory—is considered by Wolf in her essay on the "scenographic dramaturgy" of the nineteenth century; Carney regards Boucicault's strategy of gender doubling and its effect on the American theatre. Kippola examines the alterations made by Edwin Forrest to the script of Jack Cade to create a vehicle for himself, simultaneously silencing the female characters and transforming the politics of the piece, and Holland applies contemporary theory of gender "lenses" to the female characters in *The Black Crook*.

Nineteenth-century concern with selling gender as a commodity took several forms. Marti LoMonaco looks at the career of Lulu Glaser at the turn of the twentieth century and her performance of ultrafemininity in her comic opera roles; Sherry Caldwell extends actresses' embodiment of womanhood beyond the physical theatre to the wider cultural stage of advertisements in her examination of the employment of performers in the sale of personal products. Helen Huff considers benefit performances by women as a kind of gendered community in which roles and works not usually offered in regular repertoires were enacted. Roger Hall's study of cross-dressing as a convention in frontier plays spotlights the career of Gowongo Mohawk, and Kirsten Pullen juxtaposes the performances of Charlotte Cushman and Lydia Thompson in their cross-dressed roles as the major stars of the legitimate and illegitimate stages, respectively. The volume concludes with an excerpt of the transcript of the closing discussion among guest speakers Susan Cole, Elizabeth Reitz Mullenix, and Lisa Merrill.

I would particularly like to thank my predecessor, John Countryman, and Tom Stephens, of Randolph-Macon Woman's College, for graciously hosting a stimulating conference; former editor John Frick for his friendship and advice; Robin Armstrong for her extraordinary assistance to me in planning the symposium; and Lindy Bumgarner for her superb editorial assistance in the assembly of the publication.

NOREEN BARNES-MCLAIN
Virginia Commonwealth University

Suppressing the Female Voice

Edwin Forrest's Silencing of
Women in *Jack Cade*

Karl Kippola

ROBERT T. CONRAD'S *JACK CADE* has garnered what little attention it has received through its connection to the first great American actor, Edwin Forrest. Summarily dismissed by the few scholars that address it as merely another one of Forrest's prizewinners restating the ideals of Jacksonian democracy and republican freedom, *Jack Cade* is, in fact, the only one of Forrest's contest-winning plays that had received prior production, having won an award in 1841 after a moderately successful initial run in Philadelphia in 1835.[1] Between the 1835 and 1841 productions the script underwent significant changes that transformed it from a piece of Whig propaganda that reflected a strong Gothic influence into a simplistic ode to Jacksonian manhood.

No one has yet attempted a close comparison of Conrad's 1835 text (which will henceforth be distinguished as Conrad's *Aylmere*) and the 1841 Forrest-inspired/dictated *Jack Cade*.[2] The most significant challenge in such a comparison lies in differentiating between changes made purely to streamline the play for more effective production and changes made because they might have been at odds with the Jacksonian message, Forrest's narrowly defined self-image, or the desired social agenda. Beyond the overt political message, the differences between the 1835 and 1841 texts offer insights into the construction and treatment of women on the nineteenth-century American stage. In particular the treatment of Mariamne and Kate—both of whom face would-be rapists with courage and defiance in Conrad's original script but are silenced in Forrest's version of the play—provide a central focus for my discussion.

In this essay I use *Jack Cade* to explore the changing perception of women on the American stage in the early nineteenth century, suggesting that the "silencing" of Kate and Mariamne reflects the triumph of aggressive Jacksonian males over submissive women who cry out for protection and domination. I also suggest that the concept of rape held different yet vital symbolic meanings for Forrest and Conrad and that changes made to the script reveal divergent interpretations of the act. In Conrad's *Aylmere* the threat of sexual violation connotes destruction of the community. Kate and Mariamne, in their acts of resistance, inspire and empower those around them. The women's sexual identity and individuality remain significant elements of the story. In Forrest's *Jack Cade*, however, the women are reduced to ciphers and the rapes to symbolic efforts to "emasculate" the Jacksonian hero, Jack Cade, by victimizing and destroying his sexual "property." These contrasting views of rape and sexuality typify the outlook of the respective social and political allegiances of Forrest and Conrad.

Robert T. Conrad (1810–58) trained for a legal career but had a profound interest in both journalism and literature.[3] He edited the *Philadelphia Gazette,* a highly respected and influential Whig periodical; the *North American,* a popular Philadelphia newspaper soon to become a significant national Whig mouthpiece; and *Graham's Magazine,* a literary magazine that encouraged the development of American literature. Conrad became the first elected mayor of consolidated Philadelphia in 1854, running as a candidate for the combined Whig and American parties and strongly supporting the nationalist policies of the Know-Nothing party. Conrad was called "something of a genius as a poet and dramatist" and was said to occupy "the first place among our Philadelphia literati," exposing a strong connection with a primarily elite audience.[4]

Edwin Forrest (1806–72), America's first native-born star, rose to popularity through the adoration and support of working-class audiences. Forrest demanded roles that enabled him to showcase his strengths and to define himself as a symbol of American nationalism—a true Jacksonian hero of the people. Forrest was a staunch Democrat and a friend and fan of Andrew Jackson, actively supporting and campaigning for him. Forrest spoke at a national convention for Jackson's successor,

Martin Van Buren, and even received an offer from the New York Democratic Republican Nominating Committee to run for state representative. Forrest's "deeply rooted patriotic fervor demanded that he force the theatre to serve the cause of democracy."[5] Forrest's playwriting competitions sought a truly American drama, and *Jack Cade* was Forrest's last successful contest winner.

Both versions of the play follow roughly the same plot outline and are based on the Peasant Rebellion of 1450, a relatively minor revolt of Kentish bondmen led by Jack Cade.[6] Before the action of the play Cade's father, a bondman, strikes Lord Say, for which he is condemned and scourged to death. In retaliation the young Cade strikes Say and flees to Italy. The plot of Conrad's 1835 version begins ten years later with a bleak view of the cruelly oppressed bondmen. Keeping a promise made to his mother, Cade returns to Kent (with a wife, Mariamne, and young son) disguised as Dr. Aylmere, revealing his vow to God to free the bondmen. While Cade plots insurrection with the villeins, the evil Say burns Cade's home and kills his mother. Cade and his family are forced to hide in the forest, where his son dies of hunger; when Cade is forced to beg for food, he is captured by Say, and his wife goes mad and is imprisoned after killing a would-be rapist. Cade escapes and leads the rebel forces into London, demanding the delivery of Say and a signed charter freeing the bondmen. Cade kills Say but not before Cade is struck by Say's poisoned dagger. Cade's mad wife dies in his arms, and as the sealed charter is delivered, he dies.

An important subplot follows the wedding of a young local couple—Will Mowbray, a yeoman, and Kate Worthy, daughter of a blacksmith. Lord Say's steward, Courtnay, who also woos Kate, threatens their happy nuptials and convinces Say to forbid the wedding: "I'd force this blacksmith knave give up his daughter, if but to teach him that he is my thrall, even yeoman though he be."[7] As the village defiantly continues with the wedding plans, a drunken Courtnay attempts to rape Kate, but her father beats Courtnay to death with his blacksmith hammer. This attack on Kate galvanizes the bondmen, sparking the revolt.

In the world of Conrad's play women are presented as strong, vocal, and active members of the community. The attempted rapes of the drama's principal women, Mariamne and Kate, serve as catalysts to inspire rebellion against the tyranny of aristocratic rule. The perceived class distinctions between the seducer and the seduced (Kate is a child of the villein class, and Mariamne, although socially elevated, is disguised as a woman of the village) underscore the injustice of the social and political system and parallel the domination of the lords over the bondmen. Although emphasizing these class distinctions, Conrad was not supporting the antebellum class-based view of womanhood, which attributed promiscuity to the lower classes.[8] Mariamne and Kate are both presented as strong, noble, and virtuous.

Forrest's 1841 version cuts the scene that introduces Kate—a light and comic prenuptial celebration reminiscent in tone of the pastoral shepherd scenes in Shakespeare's *A Winter's Tale*—and that presents Kate as a less-educated but more spirited personification of Perdita. Her impish teasing of the prospective bridegroom ("I must ever have my way!"), in which she interprets the marriage contract as free license to disruptive behavior, subtly parallels the bondmen's demands for their rights under the charter: "Will, remember! 'Tis i' the contract that I shall be shrewish. If there be murmuring, thou shalt be so spur-galled. I'll beat thee, Will, i' faith!"[9]

Forrest's elimination of this introduction reduces the initial impression of Kate at the wedding festival to that of a bland and passive victim. Her single protest against her marriage to Will in the following scene, without the context of her earlier comic objections, is vaguely disconcerting—suggesting the marriage is truly against her will and indicating that she may be a victim of the village villeins as well as of the aristocratic villains. The bondmen praise her simple goodness and condemn Courtnay's lecherous advances. Kate, however, is no longer presented as a strong, vibrant young woman who will not be dominated; instead, she becomes almost an afterthought—little more than a plot device providing a rallying point, a catalyst for the dissatisfaction of the bondmen against the unnatural privileges of the aristocracy, and a symbol of the pure and passive Jacksonian ideal of womanhood. When Say and Courtnay interrupt the marriage festival, Forrest removes the most forceful of her efforts to restrain her father and bridegroom: "Thou'lt not deny me now. I know thou wilt not."[10] Kate is reduced to a weak, pleading damsel in distress.

In both versions of the text Kate is stunned into silence after Courtnay's attempted rape and his brutal murder. In Conrad's *Aylmere* the killing of the carefree, vital spirit within the "merry madcap" is a tragedy. This death of hope and happiness makes an armed rebellion against the aristocracy a moral imperative. The men of the village will fight to the death to avenge this outrage. In Forrest's *Jack Cade* the violence silences a woman whose voice has already been muted. Rather than driving the bondmen into vengeful action, the attack on the purity of their silent daughter fills them with impotent rage. In Forrest's revision the rape of Kate is used as a tool to show the degeneration of society and the necessity of a great Jacksonian commander, a hero personified in Forrest, to pull the passionate but powerless bondmen out from under their oppressive yoke and lead them to freedom.

Cade's wife, Mariamne, is not silenced to the same extreme as Kate Worthy, but her role is similarly diminished in size, strength, and significance in Forrest's version. In Conrad's *Aylmere* Mariamne's voice is first heard in a private discussion with Cade in which she questions his devotion to her in the face of his firm resolve to free the bondmen, "ere we grew / Sad of love's gentle troubles." She expresses her concern for his safety and the bondmen against the armies of the aristocracy: "In the wild war, / Thou and thy friends are kindling." Conrad's Mariamne fights to overcome Cade's stubborn resolve, appealing to her husband and father of her son, who brought her into this strange land, and expresses a premonition of the danger to come: "Trifle not with my fears. I am alone. Nor kith, nor country have I, hope nor stay, save thee, my husband. Ponder not so wildly on these stern doings!"[11]

The strength behind these arguments and warnings is eliminated from Forrest's *Jack Cade*. Mariamne is left to pine for happy, carefree days in Italy and to plead weakly with her husband to run from danger: "Fly with me from this place and these wild projects!" Her submission to his decision is the same in both versions, but without the passion of her earlier resolve to rescue her husband and family, the surrender of Forrest's heroine seems vapid and inane: " 'Twere delight to share A peaceful lot with thee; but if fate wills The storm should gather o'er thee,—be it so, By thy dear side I'll think it sunshine, Aylmere!"[12] Because Mariamne does not provide an obstacle of weight or substance to her husband's single-minded quest for freedom, Forrest's Cade is presented as an unquestioned master of both his family and his country.

When Mariamne is first accosted by Clifford, her aristocratic would-be rapist, she defends herself and her honor by showing a strength of resolve and spirit that betrays the privileged nature of her station: "Pass on in thy base hunt! Here thou'lt find pride even prouder than thine own, and scorn to which thy scorn is lowliness!"[13] This passage is removed from Forrest's adaptation, so Mariamne's self-defense is reduced to a plea for gentleman-like behavior and respect for womanhood: "that name entitled to / Each true man's courtesy."[14] This weak plea, which must inevitably be ignored by the callous aristocrat, serves to reinforce the image of woman as helpless victim.

Clifford initially sees Mariamne as little more than a rustic conquest: "The flower I'd cull / Is fresh and fair and coy." When Mariamne rebukes him, presenting herself as a woman of stature and substance, his ardor only grows: "If in thy cloud I thought thee bright, forgive me, / That now, thou shin'st undimmed—I worship thee." He is exhilarated, defying the taboo of seducing a woman of his class under the guise of sport with a country wench. As he prepares to accost Mariamne in prison, Conrad presents Clifford's only significant moment of pause: "Will not my name / Rot in the foulness of this villain deed?"[15] Forrest's elimination of this passage diminishes the significance and atrocity of the rape and strengthens the class-based view of women as inconsequential and submissive victims.

When the lustful Clifford attempts seduction by force, Mariamne kills him with the knife her husband has given her. In Conrad's play Aylmere gives her the knife to allow her to save herself from potential danger in his absence: "Be it, what I cannot be—thy protector!" In Forrest's version—in a speech rewritten by Forrest himself—he presents the knife as a tool for Mariamne to free herself from the lurking danger of dishonor by turning it on *herself*: "In peril's hour, be it thy refuge!"[16] Conrad's Cade places Mariamne's personal safety, security, and well-being above all; Forrest requires death before dishonor—*her* death before *his* dishonor.

In Conrad's *Aylmere* Mariamne plunges the knife into her would-be rapist, shouting, "This for Aylmere! . . . For mine honour, this—and this!" Forrest discards the second half of her outcry; and in the final line of the scene, as the last words she utters before descending into madness, Forrest adds, " 'Twas for thy [Aylmere's] honour, I did strike the blow."[17] Rape is no longer presented as a devastating physical and emotional nightmare for Mariamne but rather as a blow to the honor and ego of Cade. Mariamne's personal investment in the act is diminished, if not eliminated. No events are allowed to have any gravity or consequence outside of the impact on the psyche or aspirations of the male hero. Conrad's version of the play intimates that a woman's honor rests within herself and is her own to defend, whereas Forrest assumes a masculine proprietorship of female virtue, suggesting that the act of marriage demands that a woman relinquish not only her right to virtue but also her right to defend it.[18]

The mad scene in which Mariamne escapes from Lord Say's camp is entirely cut from Forrest's *Jack Cade*. This omission is likely, at least in part, because it is a show-stealing feature for the actress that would inevitably take focus from the tragic and adventurous plight of the hero. Also, the loss of this scene does not significantly mar the overall construction of the plot. There are, however, some intriguing references within the delirium of her madness. Early in the scene she fantasizes about her home in Italy: "Its breath / Visits my forehead like a mother's kiss." And later, after her attendants have run off, she exclaims: "Now this is joyous! No eye gazes on me! My spirit-loves, my mother and my sisters, Will now come to me.—Men say I am mad, I, mad! A merry thought. (Laughs.) Come, mother, come and speak to me!"[19]

Madness is presented as a male-constructed horror that can only be combated or assuaged through a connection with the female, and Mariamne is systematically stripped of her feminine bond and the various aspects of her feminine identity. She has watched the Widow Cade, her only mother figure, beaten and burned to death. (Forrest even eliminated a brief scene early in the play between Mariamne and the Widow Cade that established a soft and emotional family bond.) Mariamne has watched her son slowly die of starvation, and his death terminates her maternal identity. The attempted rape has challenged and called into question the essence of her femininity, her virtue. And she was forced to defend herself by killing, in a decidedly masculine manner, the one who would have taken her womanhood. Although Mariamne has lost all connection to the feminine, both internal and external, the madness-inducing terror of this realization exists only in Conrad's world.

Conrad constantly uses the suffering and dishonor of women as a catalyst for male action. The martyred immolation of the Widow Cade incites Cade into active rebellion against the aristocracy. The attempted rape of Kate sparks the first murder of an aristocrat at the hands of a bondman and spurs the village men to action. The attempted rape, subsequent madness, and eventual death of Mariamne serve to strengthen Cade's resolve, justifying what might otherwise be considered harsh or unjust behavior. Cade even callously goads a reluctant and peaceful bondman with the memory of his recently deceased wife to force him into joining the fight: "I could weep for thee, / And thy wife murdered, save that tears kill not." The response? "The tears shed for her shall be red and heart-drawn!"[20]

Conrad has created strong, complex female characters that are marginalized and diminished on Forrest's stage. Conrad's original play presents heroines in a fully dimensional Shakespearean mold; his story centers on ingenuous and imperiled women who are empowered through their struggle against aristocratic foes. Forrest's adaptation purges these

Gothic elements and reduces the women, psychologically and dramatically, to stock melodrama characters, refocusing the anguish of the rape experience on the man rather than the woman. Women serve as a commodity, as chattel—a source of male honor, and as a key to male domination.

During the antebellum period, responses to rape and seduction depended entirely on the status and reputation of the victim. Women of the upper classes were rarely even asked to testify in rape cases, keeping their reputations intact, whereas women of the lower classes ran a serious risk of humiliation and loss of reputation and could expect little sympathy or legal redress. The Philadelphia Magdalen Society, founded in 1800 to address the problem of prostitution, initially viewed its female charges (most of whom had working-class backgrounds) as victims of lechery, but by the 1840s there was "a complete inversion of the initial discourse of the Society's founders," who "justified their work with prostitutes not as a means to save vulnerable young women, but as a means to help young men whom prostitutes placed at risk."[21]

Seduction novels of the period, in which seduction was seen as a product of the male's animal lust and the female's innocence and "passionlessness," featured "women victims [primarily of the upper classes] who typically suffered from madness or death after lustful men ruined them." Seduction was invariably presented as a crime against both the woman and the family, if not the entire community. As Cathy N. Davidson so persuasively argues in her analysis of the seduction novel *The Power of Sympathy:* "But it must also be emphasized that seduction . . . is a metaphor not just of women's status in the Republic but of a range of problems, all of which might be reduced to the same structure or seduction plot—that is, a range of problems that arise when moral value and social responsibility are outweighed by the particular desires, no matter how basely self-serving, of privileged individuals or classes."[22] Forrest's reduction of the importance of women and the significance of their sexual violation ultimately softens the blow and mutes the call to arms against the tyranny and oppression of the aristocracy. Forrest transforms Conrad's play about the outrage of a united community into a melodrama depicting the painful struggle of one man against insurmountable odds.

The passion, strength, and Jacksonian masculinity of Forrest's performances (of this story and others) created clear binaries between good and evil, man and woman, leader and follower—essentially eliminating the need for the audience to think or take action. This reductive and simplified storytelling may explain why so many historians lump Forrest's plays together. Jacksonians had a strong and clear conception of ideal masculinity and two alluring, dominant, and inspiring models in Jackson and Forrest.

The Whigs, however, lacked this clear masculine definition and searched for a male identity distinct from, if not opposite to, their Jacksonian rivals. The Whigs were in an awkward transitional moment. The early republic had found the country in the hands of a wealthy and educated elite. The first generation of America's leaders could always invoke their immediate connection to the myth of George Washington as the quintessential man of the people, but once that generation died, much of the Whig connection to the working people of the country was severed. The Whigs could not create or assume a masculine identity in stark contrast to the strength and indomitable spirit of the Democratic Republicans that did not condemn the Whigs as effete, ineffectual, and hopelessly disconnected from the people.[23] The Whigs lacked a truly masculine hero and identity, which may explain why Conrad's version of the story asserted the community as hero rather than relying on a solitary Napoleonic figure.

It is only through suppressing the female voice that *Jack Cade* achieved its phenomenal success in the Jacksonian period, becoming one of Forrest's most performed roles and among the period's most popular plays. Once *Jack Cade* was reconfigured to conform to Forrest's presentation of Jacksonian masculinity, as well as to the shifting notions of female virtue, it "spoke" to an American audience. It is ironic that Forrest was compelled to silence one group in order to speak to another. His manipulation of Conrad's text brings to vivid life the warning of Abigail Adams: "All men would be tyrants if they could."[24]

Notes

1. The comparisons of *Jack Cade* to Forrest's other popular prizewinners, *Metamora* and *The Gladiator,* are too numerous to list here. The following are three significant and representative examples: Montrose J. Moses, ed., *Representative American Plays by American Dramatists from 1765 to the Present Day,* vol. 2, *1815–1858* (New York: Benjamin Blom, 1925), 427–30; Gary A. Richardson, "Plays and Playwrights: 1800–1865," in *The Cambridge History of American Theatre,* vol. 1, *Beginnings to 1870,* ed. Don B. Wilmeth and Christopher Bigsby (Cambridge: Cambridge University Press, 1998), 267–70; Bruce A. McConachie, *Melodramatic Formations: American Theatre and Society, 1820–1870* (Iowa City:

University of Iowa Press, 1992), 97–110. These comparisons have of necessity been rather perfunctory and, in some cases, not entirely accurate, failing to take many social and political factors into account.

2. Conrad's play was initially produced as *Aylmere, or The Bondman of Kent.* Forrest originally performed the play under that title but, at the encouragement of theatre manager Francis Courtney Wemyss, quickly changed it to *Jack Cade; or, The Noble Yeoman,* and it was under that title that the play achieved its significant national popularity.

3. Biographical information on the life of Conrad is taken from the following sources: Moses, *Representative Plays,* 427–38; Allen Johnson and Dumas Malone, eds., *Dictionary of American Biography* (New York: Charles Scribner's Sons, 1958), 2:355–56; Joseph Jackson, *Literary Landmarks of Philadelphia* (Philadelphia: David McKay, 1939), 70–73; Ellis Paxson Oberholtzer, *The Literary History of Philadelphia* (Philadelphia: George W. Jacobs, 1906), 246–49.

4. Jackson, *Literary Landmarks,* 70; Edgar Allan Poe, "A Chapter on Autobiography," *Graham's Magazine,* June 1841, 281.

5. Richard Moody, *Edwin Forrest: First Star of the American Stage* (New York: Alfred A. Knopf, 1960), 87. Forrest's connection to Jacksonian Democracy and its influence on his stage work is most effectively discussed in Bruce A. McConachie, "The Theatre of Edwin Forrest and Jacksonian Hero Worship," in *When They Weren't Doing Shakespeare: Essays on Nineteenth-Century British and American Theatre,* ed. Judith L. Fisher and Stephen Watt (Athens: University of Georgia Press, 1989).

6. Shakespeare uses a combination of the most sensational elements of the uprising led by Jack Cade and Wat Tyler's Peasants' Rebellion of 1381 to inspire the Jack Cade comic subplot in *Henry VI,* part 2.

7. Robert T. Conrad, *"Aylmere, or The Bondman of Kent"; and Other Poems* (Philadelphia: E. H. Butler, 1852), 72. A great deal of pride existed in the yeoman title during this period, reflecting the real or imagined Arcadian values of Jeffersonian republicanism, "which emphasized community solidarity, family honor, and manly independence" (McConachie, *Melodramatic Formations,* 66).

8. Rodney Hessinger, "Victim of Seduction or Vicious Woman? Conceptions of the Prostitute at the Philadelphia Magdalen Society, 1800–1850," *Exploration in Early American Culture* 66 (1999): 202; Christine Stansell, *City of Women: Sex and Class in New York, 1789–1860* (Chicago: University of Illinois Press, 1982).

9. Conrad, *Aylmere,* 20. Conrad freely mixes the comic with the serious throughout the bulk of the play. Forrest generally eliminates the lighter moments, providing a more consistently elevated tragic tone, but these adjustments also allow for less dimension in characterization and flatten the dramatic situations.

10. Ibid., 36.

11. Ibid., 55–58.

12. Robert T. Conrad, prompt copy, *Aylmere; or, The Kentish Rebellion,*

"Property of Edwin Forrest," Marked for Mr. Forrest by D. A. Sarzedas, Prompter, Park Theatre May 24th 1841 New York (University of Pennsylvania, Forrest Collection), 30, 31. For ease of reference Forrest's acting version will subsequently be abbreviated as *Jack Cade*.

13. Conrad, *Aylmere*, 66.

14. Forrest, *Jack Cade*, 36.

15. Conrad, *Aylmere*, 44, 67, 120.

16. Ibid., 119; Forrest, *Jack Cade*, 61.

17. Conrad, *Aylmere*, 125; Forrest, *Jack Cade*, 66.

18. Bruce A. McConachie details Forrest's strong views on the role of women and his divorce from Catherine Norton Sinclair in 1850 because of her alleged infidelity, which "was more a matter of public honor than private trust." Forrest saw women as "inferior . . . and hence dependent upon men," whereas his upper-class wife believed "men and women were natural equals and should work together for moral progress." Even though no evidence directly connects Forrest's reduction of the women's roles in *Jack Cade* to the personal struggles in his marriage, it is an interesting speculation. See McConachie, *Melodramatic Formations*, 71–72.

19. Conrad, *Aylmere*, 137.

20. Ibid., 80.

21. Jane H. Pease and William H. Pease, *Ladies, Women, and Wenches: Choices and Constraint in Antebellum Charleston and Boston* (Chapel Hill: University of North Carolina Press, 1990), 143; Hessinger, "Victim of Seduction," 214.

22. Nancy F. Cott, "Passionless: An Interpretation of Victorian Sexual Ideology, 1790–1850," *Signs: Journal of Women in Culture and Society* 4 (1978): 220; Patricia Cline Cohen, *The Murder of Helen Jewett: The Life and Death of a Prostitute in Nineteenth-Century New York* (New York: Vintage Books, 1998), 228; Rodney Hessinger, "Insidious Murderers of Female Innocence: Representations of Masculinity in the Seduction Tales of the Late Eighteenth Century," in *Sex and Sexuality in Early America,* ed. Merril D. Smith (New York: New York University Press, 1998), 275; Cathy N. Davidson, *Revolution and the Word: The Rise of the Novel in America* (Oxford: Oxford University Press, 1986), 108.

23. I would like to thank Albrecht Koschnik for his comments and suggestions on the question of Whig masculinity and direct the reader to his excellent study of young Federalist identity: "Fashioning a Federalist Self: Young Men and Voluntary Association in Early Nineteenth-Century Philadelphia," *Exploration in Early American Culture* 4 (2000): 218–57. Women in the early republic also struggled for identity after being at least partially integrated into civil polity through the necessities of the Revolution and after having "begun to invent an ideology of citizenship that merged the domestic domain of the pre-industrial woman with the new public ideology of individual responsibility and civic virtue" (Linda K. Kerber, *Women of the Republic: Intellect and Ideology in Revolutionary America* [New York: Norton, 1980], 269). I am not implying that

Conrad was championing the rights of women through his play, but there are at least surface similarities between the quests for identity in both women and Whigs during this period.

24. L. H. Butterfield, ed., *Adams Family Correspondence* (Cambridge, Mass.: Belknap, 1968), 1:370.

The Old Buzzard

Figuring Gender in *The Black Crook*

Dorothy Holland

T HE *BLACK CROOK* OCCUPIES a prominent place in theatre history. For many theatre historians it represents the first American musical comedy; for others its primary significance is its position as the herald of a new kind of theatrical entertainment: "the leg show."[1] When *The Black Crook* opened at Niblo's Garden on September 8, 1866, it was an immediate sensation with audiences and a box-office bonanza for its producers. Subsequent productions were mounted in major cities throughout the country, and revivals were regularly produced into the early twentieth century. The phenomenal success of *The Black Crook* was largely attributable to a corps of female dancers who, as the *New York Times* noted, wore "no clothes to speak of." "Everybody is talking about it and the many beauties it reveals to our bewildered gaze," reported the *New York Clipper*. Producers even advertised a time schedule for the show's dances so that a patron could "drop in, take a peek at his favorite scene, or dancer, or leg or something and enjoying the sight, return to the bosom of the family."[2]

The emergence of the leg show and its unprecedented commodification of the female body in the 1860s—at precisely the time when women's demands for legal, economic, and educational rights had been gaining ground—can be seen as part of a widespread retrenchment of patriarchal forces in mid-nineteenth-century America. As social historian Faye E. Dudden notes, "Even as women gained access to higher education, politics, and the upper reaches of the labor market, they and the men around them were becoming more and more immersed in entertainment products that diminished women."[3]

How does *The Black Crook* diminish women? How does it work to contain female power and sexuality, and how does it reinscribe patriarchal gender ideology and power relations? Cultural images are powerful transmitters of what psychologist Sandra Bem calls the "lenses of gender embedded in cultural discourse." Bem identifies three gender lenses that perpetuate the oppression of women and systematically reproduce male power: gender polarization, which defines "mutually exclusive scripts for being male and female . . . and defines any person or behavior that deviates from these scripts as problematic . . . unnatural . . . immoral . . . pathological"; androcentrism, which defines male as the standard and female as an inferior deviation whose value is recognized only in terms of functional significance (domestic and sexual) to the male; and biological essentialism, which "rationalizes and legitimizes both other lenses by treating them as the natural and inevitable consequences of the intrinsic biological natures of men and women."[4]

Bem's articulation of the gender lenses embedded in cultural discourse provides a useful analytical tool for investigating the ways the text and performance of *The Black Crook* contain female power and sexuality and reinscribe patriarchal gender ideology and power relations.[5] Gender polarization is reflected in the play with the naturally exclusive scripts assigned to female and male characters: females are chosen, not choosing, acted upon, not active agents, whereas male characters freely pursue their own desires and drive the narrative forward. Androcentrism operates in both the narrative focus of the play and the spectacle of performance itself; the central figure of the play is a young male; it is desire, his battle with powerful male opponents, that commands our attention. The female characters are delineated in relation to the male hero; Amina, the epitome of True Womanhood—pious, pure, submissive—is the domestic/sexual prize the hero seeks; Queen Stalacta, the embodiment of Nature, drawn as a bountiful, fecund, and potentially dangerous female power, is the hero's protector—guarding him on his journey and rewarding him with treasure at play's end. Androcentrism can also be read in the theatrical performance itself, with the spectacle of nearly one hundred silenced, scantily attired females on display for primarily male spectators.[6] Finally, biological essentialism may be seen in the production's fundamental focus on the female body. The production boldly reiterates the to-be-looked-at-ness of the female body, as well as the looking/desiring male subject. Biology is indeed destiny within the dramatic text and the theatrical performance of *The Black Crook*. The production's reiteration of these lenses of gender must be read against contesting social practices and discourse, however. Cultural tensions surrounding gender roles can be seen in two seemingly transgressive female characters.

Queen Stalacta and Dame Barbara clearly violate gender polarization

Cabinet photo of Pauline Markham as Queen Stalacta in *The Black Crook*. Harvard Theatre Collection, Houghton Library. Used by permission.

by transgressing traditional feminine scripts and exhibiting traditionally masculine actions and characteristics. Stalacta, the leader of an army of Amazons, fairies, and gnomes, is depicted as a powerful and independent female. Armed with battle-ax and shield, the popular British actress Pauline Markham displays a commanding stride as Queen Stalacta. It is not only Stalacta's appearance but also her actions that express courage and power: she rescues the young male hero not once but four times during the course of the play (2.4; 3.1; 4.2; 4.3). A female rescuing a male hero from danger does seem revolutionary; however, if we consider the context of her actions, the seemingly revolutionary is subsumed within traditional gender values. The fairy queen only saves the hero because he unknowingly saved her life: she had been turned into a dove by the archfiend Zamiel and was about to be devoured by a snake, but Rodolphe, seeing this poor trembling dove on the tree branch, struck the snake and saved her. This incident reflects traditional gender roles: she is the trembling dove, he the powerful protector. Thus, the play clearly delineates that it is only because of his protective act that the fairy queen becomes his protector. "I am still thy debtor and must ever be," says the fairy queen, reiterating a fundamental bargain in patriarchal sexual politics: female service in exchange for male protection. Because he saved her life, she is obliged to save his. "Thou art environed by danger and need the power of my protection," she says, and throughout the play Stalacta fulfills her obligation. She employs her prodigious powers only in the service of the male hero. Because his initial heroic and chivalrous act is the cause for her beneficence, her interventions and her strength in battle do not compromise the hero's manhood. Nor do they challenge the gender relations in the world beyond the footlights. Quite the contrary, at a time when urban males faced treacherous market fluctuations, widespread social changes, and threatening demands for female emancipation, this figure of independent female power can be seen as both expressing fears and at the same time subsuming those fears beneath a vision of an almost omnipotent feminine loyalty and care.[7]

Dame Barbara, played by thirty-seven-year-old Mary Wells, also seems to defy traditional female scripts.[8] She openly engages in the business of marriage negotiations with an eye only on profit, and she is unmoved by either the rhetoric of true love or the cultural ideal of maternal sacrifice. The play begins with Dame Barbara's opposition to the marriage of her foster daughter, Amina, to the young poet, Rodolphe. Reneging on her earlier promise to let the couple marry, Barbara has decided to give Amina to a higher bidder—Count Wolfenstein:

> RODOLPHE. Hark ye, Dame, I love Amina. She loves me. You yourself promised that she should be mine as I could command one hundred pounds.
> BARBARA. Pah—that was before I knew her value—but now that I do know it, and others know it too, I changed my mind.[9]

Akin to traditionally drawn male characters, Dame Barbara actively pursues her own personal advancement and desire. She is concerned with

Cabinet photo of Mary Wells. Harvard Theatre Collection, Houghton Library. Used by permission.

the benefits that she can derive from her foster daughter's marriage, and she openly expresses her own desire as she courts Count Wolfenstein's steward. As the photograph of comic actress Mary Wells suggests, Dame Barbara, with her exaggerated finery and her imperious airs, is a figure of ridicule. She is portrayed as a caricature of a material crone who simply uses her foster daughter to pursue her own social advancement, and her amorous adventures are rendered ludicrous. Barbara serves as the brunt of jokes and ridicule; her behavior and her person are held up as despicable and foolish.[10] The treatment of Dame Barbara demonstrates Sandra Bem's observation that those who violate their prescribed gender-polarized script are problematic, unnatural, immoral, pathological. Dame Barbara and Queen Stalacta actually serve as the play's most profound reiterations of patriarchal gender ideology and power relations. Dame Barbara serves as a negative example, ridiculed and scorned for her nonconformity, and Queen Stalacta serves as fantasy mediating very real fears regarding the emergence of uncontrollable female power and independence.

Significantly, the proliferation of the leg shows coincided with the emerging medical establishment's—particularly gynecology's—project to securely anchor gender roles and gender relations in biology. Given the degree of social flux and the changing nature of work at midcentury, the incursions of women in formerly male-only professions could be seen as yet another threat to masculine identity, an identity based on work in the public spheres of business, politics, and the arts. The association of public life was so firmly associated with male identity that when a woman managed a business or handled investments or sold property, she was called "a man of business" because the phrase "woman of business" was seen as an oxymoron. As the first wave of feminism broke down barriers to women's entry into the public sphere, the stability of sphere-defined masculine identity was understandably threatened, and the need arose to anchor gender in a more secure foundation—the body.[11]

The figuration of gender in *The Black Crook* involves not only the inscriptions of gender but also the inscriptions of age. The study of age as a socially constructed category of identity and difference is a relatively recent development. As Margaret Morganroth Gullette has observed: "Many formulators alert to other constructions implicitly keep in circulation the sleepy illusion that age and aging are historical, prediscursive, natural. And this can happen because age is still at the stage where gender and race used to be: hidden by its supposed foundation in 'the body.' " As Gullette insists, although "we think we are aged by nature; we are insistently and precociously being aged by culture."[12] Of course, the inscriptions of gender and age are intimately entwined, as we will see in the figuration of age and gender in *The Black Crook*.

Among the hundred-plus characters in *The Black Crook*, only Dame Barbara and the sorcerer, Hertzog, are delineated as "old." As such, their significance is profound: they serve as exemplars of old age amid a sea of youthfulness. But how old is old in mid-nineteenth-century age ideology? The answer, as medical authorities insist, depends on one's sex. Dr. George Napheys explains: "Man is man for a longer time than woman is woman, with him it is a life-time matter; with her it is but a score of years or so. Her child-bearing period is less than half her life." In other words, gender is defined by procreative ability, and, as Dr. Napheys unequivocally points out, woman stops being woman when she can no longer procreate. At menopause, roughly late forties or early fifties, woman is no longer woman. According to the medical writing of the day this change is sudden and absolute. Aging for the male, on the other hand, is seen as much more gradual, for, as Dr. Edward Tilt explains, "the impulse . . . given [at puberty] to the constitution of man by the sexual apparatus is, in general, fully effective and all sufficient to insure its permanent activity until extreme old age."[13] Indeed, these are the gendered marks of age attributed to Hertzog and Dame Barbara: although stooped and withered with extremely advanced age, the sorcerer is still a formidable adversary, whereas Barbara, somewhere in her climacteric forties as signaled by reference to hot flashes, is deemed a foolish "old buzzard."[14]

In both cases, then, villainy is predicated on age. When the withered and bent Hertzog first appears in act 1, scene 3, he fears that his life "hath well nigh run its course," and he bemoans the loss of his former powers—specifically power over other men.[15] Fearful of death and unwilling to give up his power, Hertzog appeals to the archfiend Zamiel for help. Zamiel offers to give Hertzog one year of life for every fresh, young soul that he delivers; Hertzog agrees to deliver the young hero, Rodolphe. Likewise Dame Barbara is shown to have lost her female power (physical attractiveness):

Barbara enters, extravagantly dressed, wearing a monstrous cap ridiculously trimmed.
BARBARA. There! Having complete her Ladyship's toilet, I have attended

to my own, and if I know anything about dress, I flatter myself that my appearance would do honor to any occasion.[16]

Needless to say, her appearance evokes mockery, not honor. To get the attention and honor that she desires, Barbara barters her only asset—her youthful foster daughter, Amina.

Thus both Hertzog and Dame Barbara engage in contemptible commercial exchanges: Hertzog selling the soul of the hero, Dame Barbara selling the body of the heroine. As exemplars of old age within the world of the play, they present a striking figuration of generational antagonism and distrust, with the elder generation surviving at the expense of the younger.

Cultural historians have identified an increase in ageism that took place in American society in the latter half of the nineteenth century. They trace changes in attitudes toward older people moving from respect to depreciation with an emergent valorization of youthfulness and demonization of old(er) age. Women, they note, were targets of these negative attitudes and associations even more so than men.[17] This differentiation is evident in the characterizations of Hertzog and Dame Barbara: whereas Hertzog is delineated as a formidable and feared villain, Dame Barbara is depicted as completely ridiculous, the brunt of jokes.

Dame Barbara's primary function is to serve as a foil to the young female bodies on display in this "leg show" extravaganza. Their "beauty" is affirmed in juxtaposition to her purported "ugliness," their youth to her age, their fertility in contradistinction to her barrenness. This contrast is articulated in the play's imagery, dialogue, and dramatic action. For example, consider the fluid imagery in this description of Queen Stalacta's grotto, the space where the scantily clad chorines perform their audience-enrapturing dances: "The Grotto of the Golden Stalactites. A grand and comprehensive water-cavern of gold, deeply perspective, with stalactiform, arched roof. Vistas, running parallel and harmonizing with the main Grotto, the mouth of which discloses an open lake and distant shore at the back. Transparent silver waters, in which are seen sporting fishes and nondescript amphibea. Diminutive fairies asleep on the waters of the Grotto in golden shells. Ground, on shore piece, richly studded with gold and jewels."[18] This is a dazzling, fertile, life-sustaining scene.

Compare the fluid imagery of the grotto with that describing Dame Barbara: "I took you for a gentle spice," says Von Puffengruntz, "a sort of seasoning to the dull life I lead here in the castle, but, damn it, Madame, you have turned out to be all the condiments in one. A bottom layer of mustard, a top dressing of cayenne pepper, and a subterranean lake of vinegar." Dame Barbara is figured as an exemplar of all that is repulsive, stagnant, and lifeless. Throughout the production ridicule is aimed at her physical body, at the signs of aging—full waist, wrinkles, shortness of breath, and hot flashes. Age itself is made abhorrent in her person, and age-inappropriate behavior—feminine sexual display—is severely mocked. Significantly, the agent for the older woman's ridicule is a young female character, Carline.

When Dame Barbara displays herself in her finery, Carline observes, "Why, she looks for all the world like a great horned owl dressed up in cast-off finery of a peacock. Ha-ha-ha, did you ever?" Then, in an aside to one of the maidens, Carline says, "Observe me tickle the old buzzard," and she proceeds with the evening's sport:

> CARLINE. Why you've almost taken my breath. I declare, Dame, you're looking gorgeous. So young and girlish, too. Indeed, if I were 'Mina . . . I wouldn't care to have you in the way when his Lordship, the Count, arrives.
> BARBARA. And why not, pray?
> CARLINE. Because I should consider you a dangerous rival.

As Carline and the maidens laugh among themselves, Dame Barbara muses, "It is strange, I never noticed it before. But that girl Carline is a very sensible person." The gullible Dame remains an easy mark for Carline, and Carline continues to tickle "the old buzzard" at every opportunity.[19]

The function of the older female as a foil to the younger fosters an important visual economy in *The Black Crook:* the specter of a repugnant, older female body serves as a visual pariah, a bogey, enticing young women into the pleasure-power field of being looked at. In other words the ridiculed older female body is a fundamental linchpin for the operation of the male gaze and the enculturation of young women into the orientation of display for male viewing subjects. Furthermore, Carline and other village maidens (along with the young female spectators invited to identify with them) perpetuate the very ageism that seals their own future. The completion/obliteration articulated by Carline on the body of the older female secures a short-term triumph for Carline and the other young females, but they doom themselves at the same time. Dame Barbara's fate is ultimately their fate, for none of the young females can avoid aging. The cultural currency they claim at Dame Barbara's expense will be paid for in their own loss of cultural capital in time, and the irony is that the system ensuring that loss is reiterated in the very act of claiming those short-term benefits.

Another effect of the ageism reflected in the figuration of the old buzzard is that it serves to undermine coalition politics among generations of women. For the defenders of Victorian American gender ideals, the undermining of female coalition politics was a tactical imperative. The most prominent leaders of the women's movement in 1866 were women the age of Dame Barbara: Susan B. Anthony (age 46), Antoinette Blackwell (age 41), Amelia Bloomer (age 48), Julia Ward Howe (age 47), Elizabeth Cady Stanton (age 51), Lucy Stone (age 48). In coalition with women from previous and later generations, including Lucretia Mot (age 73), Sojourner Truth (age 69), Anna Howard Shaw (age 19), and the young Harriet Stanton (age 11), these midlife women stood at the forefront of the movement for women's rights.

Throughout history the success of the women's movement has been directly related to the effective power of coalition politics across generations of women. Likewise, its failures can be traced to the failure of coalition. Viewed in this light, the seemingly innocuous comic scenes between Dame Barbara and the coquettish Carline take on added historical significance. If we were to examine the age/gender ideology in the seemingly innocuous products of popular culture today, would we find that the twenty-first century box-office bonanzas undermine or strengthen coalition politics among women? Do the lenses of gender entwine with lenses of age to empower or disempower women in our own time?

Notes

1. Credit for prompting the "leg show" boom of the 1860s should actually go to actress/manager Laura Keene, who, in an effort to compete with the increasing popularity of the concert saloons, incorporated a corps of scantily clad females into her musical extravaganzas. Keene's burlesque spectacle *The Seven Sisters* (1860) predates *The Black Crook* by six years and was followed by two other burlesque spectacles that featured female bodies in revealing flesh-colored tights: *Seven Sons* (1861) and *Blondette* (1862). There is a significant difference between Keene's productions and *The Black Crook*, however. Keene's

productions of *The Seven Sisters* and *The Seven Sons* feature all-female casts with females performing as male characters, reflecting the traditions of breeches performance and classical burlesque, with its female transgressiveness and empowerment. For a discussion of the transgressive possibilities in burlesque and breeches performance see Robert C. Allen, *Horrible Prettiness: Burlesque and American Culture* (Chapel Hill: University of North Carolina Press, 1991); and Elizabeth Reitz Mullenix, *Wearing the Breeches: Gender on the Antebellum Stage* (New York: St. Martin's, 2000).

2. *New York Times,* review of *The Black Crook,* Sept. 13, 1866, 4; *New York Clipper,* review of *The Black Crook,* Sept. 22, 1866, 190; Leigh George Odom, "*The Black Crook* at Niblo's," *Drama Review* 26, no. 1 (spring 1982): 23–24.

3. Faye E. Dudden, *Women in American Theatre* (New Haven, Conn.: Yale University Press, 1994), 183. Interestingly, there was another innovation in the public display of scantily clad female bodies when women gained the right to vote in 1920: the Miss America pageant was created. See Jennifer Jones, "The Beauty Queen as Sacrificial Victim," *Theatre History Studies* 18 (1998): 99–106.

4. Sandra Bem, *Lenses of Gender: Transforming the Debate on Gender Inequality* (New Haven, Conn.: Yale University Press, 1993), 81, 2.

5. For those unfamiliar with *The Black Crook,* a short synopsis may be helpful: A poor young artist, Rodolphe, is betrothed to the beautiful Amina, but Rodolphe has not earned enough money to claim his bride; meanwhile, the evil Count Wolfenstein has taken an interest in Amina, and Dame Barbara (Amina's foster mother) decides to give Amina to the count. The play depicts Rodolphe's battle to rescue Amina from the evil count and to avoid being killed by the count's henchmen. The sorcerer Hertzog (a.k.a. The Black Crook) is also a threat to Rodolphe. To prolong his own life, the withered and deformed old sorcerer makes a pact with the archfiend Zamiel. Hertzog will get one year of life for every young soul he delivers to the archfiend. The first life that Zamiel wants is Rodolphe's. Fortunately, Rodolphe comes under the protection of the beautiful fairy queen Stalacta. Comic scenes involve Dame Barbara, Von Puffengruntz (the count's corpulent steward), Carline (a girl from the village who continually ridicules Dame Barbara), and Greppo (the Black Crook's drudge and, later, willing servant to Rodolphe). The play ends with Hertzog dragged down to hell, his own life forfeited because he did not succeed in getting a fresh young soul for Zamiel. The young lovers are reunited in the grand finale—an elaborate transformation scene in Queen Stalacta's Grotto of the Golden Realm.

6. It should be noted that the audience was not entirely male. Although advertisements were primarily geared to male persons, and the spectacle onstage clearly appealed to male, heterosexual interest, women also flocked to see this theatrical sensation.

7. Charles Barras, *The Black Crook,* in *"The Black Crook" and Other Nineteenth-Century American Plays,* ed. Myron Matlaw (New York: E. P. Dutton, 1967), 357.

8. According to Wells's obituary she was born in 1829. See clippings file, Billy Rose Theatre Collection, New York Public Library.

9. Barras, *Black Crook*, 327.

10. Dame Barbara's function as negative example of womanhood is perhaps an obvious counterexpression of the prevailing gender ideology, yet she embodies a more subtle function as well: she serves as a cover for the actual commodification of female flesh occurring in the production itself. Dame Barbara draws criticism for turning a young woman (Amina) into a commodity—the very criticism that could be leveled at producers William Wheatly, Henry Barrett, and Harry Palmer.

11. For examples of women identified as "men of business" see Lisa Wilson, *Life after Death: Widows in Pennsylvania, 1750–1850* (Philadelphia: Temple University Press, 1992). An example of gynecology's anchoring of gender roles in the body can be seen in the following excerpt from a lecture by Dr. Charles D. Meigs:

> She—the female—possesses that strange compound . . . ovarian stroma . . . an organ so small, so unobvious, is endued with the vast responsibility of keeping up the living scheme of the world. . . . Think of that great power —and ask your own judgments whether such an organ can be of little influence on the constitution of woman; whether she was not made in order that it should be made. . . . [H]er ovary is her sex. . . . [S]he is peculiar because of, and in order that she might have this great, this dominant organ concealed within her body. (Charles D. Meigs, *Lectures on Some of the Distinctive Characteristics of the Female* [Philadelphia: T. K. and P. G. Collins, 1847], 18)

Here we can see how biological essentialism serves not only as a lens of gender productions, as Bem points out, but also as a lens of age production, specifically as biologically determined accelerated aging for females. Borrowing Bem's model of gender lenses, I contend that there are similar lenses through which age ideology is communicated and perpetuated. The three lenses of age can be identified as follows: age polarization, which defines mutually exclusive scripts for being young and old and defines any person or behavior that deviates from these scripts as problematic, unnatural, immoral, pathological; youth centrism, which defines youthfulness as the standard and old age as an inferior deviation whose value is recognized only in terms of its functional significance to the young; and ideological essentialism, which rationalizes and legitimizes both other lenses by treating them as the natural and inevitable consequences of the intrinsic biological nature. These lenses of age operate as seemingly transparent determinants of age-appropriate life scripts and behaviors, as assumptions of youthfulness as the norm, with old age as abnormal or deviant, and they attempt to justify and ground age polarization and youth centrism as being based in "natural" body processes.

12. Margaret Morganroth Gullette, *Declining to Decline: Cultural Combat and the Politics of Midlife* (Charlottesville: University Press of Virginia, 1997), 202, 6, 7.

13. George H. Napheys, *The Physical Life of Owen: Advice to the Maiden, Wife, and Mother* (Philadelphia: H. C. Watts, 1873), 38; Edward John Tilt, *The Change of Life* (Philadelphia: Lindsay and Blakiston, 1871), 19–20.

14. Barras, *Black Crook,* 329.

15. Ibid., 334.

16. Ibid., 329.

17. See Andrew Achenbaum, *Old Age in the New Land: The American Experience since 1790* (Baltimore: Johns Hopkins University Press, 1978); Bryan S. Green, *Gerontology and the Construction of Old Age* (New York: Aldine De Gruyter, 1993).

18. Barras, *Black Crook,* 349.

19. Ibid., 369, 329. One of the show's hit songs, "You Naughty, Naughty Men," was sung by Milly Cavendish (Carline) and played across the footlights to the "bald heads" in the front rows. Carline's direct address not only would entice spectators into the scopophilic field but also would draw in and implicate spectators in the collective ridicule of the old buzzard, Dame Barbara. See Deane L. Root, *American Popular Stage Music, 1860–1880* (Ann Arbor: UMI Research Press, 1981), 94–96; Odom, "*Black Crook* at Niblo's," 35.

In Her Place

A Consideration of Gendered Space in Nineteenth-Century Melodrama

Laurie Wolf

I SSUES OF GENDER and theatrical space were predominant concerns in the production of nineteenth-century melodrama. During the Victorian period American thinking on questions of gender and sexuality was influenced by European perceptions, which found expression on the stage. "The new category of the 'public man' and his 'virtue' was constructed via a series of oppositions to 'femininity,' which both mobilised older conceptions of domesticity and women's place and rationalised them into a formal claim concerning women's nature."[1] Notions of gender and the appropriate spheres within which each existed were embedded in Victorian consciousness and manifested themselves throughout dramatic texts—in the dramaturgy as well as in scenographic descriptions. This awareness of spatial propriety was present in plays written by both women and men. I will argue that nineteenth-century writers were bound by their cultural ideologies, regardless of the gender of the writer, and were unable to write outside of their ideological framework. The two plays I will examine are Tom Taylor's *The Ticket-of-Leave Man* (1863) and William Henry Smith's *The Drunkard* (1844). Although male playwrights wrote both plays, I do not believe that there was a deliberate construction or manipulation of women's space. I suggest those differences between the public and private spheres, and the consequences to those who transgress their appointed place, are woven into the fabric of Victorian culture. Although these plays concentrate on the fall and eventual rise of their male heroes, Bob Brierly and Edward Middleton respectively, and deal specifically with their weaknesses, I will focus on the principal female characters in each —May in *The Ticket-of-Leave Man* and Mary in *The Drunkard*.

During the mid-nineteenth century the overriding belief was that male privilege was fundamental to maintaining the existing order—as had been believed for hundreds of years. Legally, this meant that women were not regarded as autonomous subjects but were always under the control of a male—father, husband, brother, or son. A woman's social identity was defined primarily by her marital status—which was also affected by her reproductive potential. The political climate began to change during the nineteenth and early twentieth centuries, however, and these changes would ultimately provide women with more educational and professional opportunities, voting rights, and other options in determining their own lives. Nevertheless, the process was painfully slow, and there were many obstacles. As women gained power and status, a majority of male cultural observers and critics did not view this as a long-overdue recasting of gender roles but as a decline in masculine virtues.

In the various definitions of gender roles throughout history, one of the great theories was that biology was destiny, that women were immeasurably different from men because they had different sex organs, functions, and feelings. Various nineteenth-century experts argued that Nature had become specialized as one moved up the chain of existence: men were designed to protect and were given the courage and endurance for that function. Women, on the other hand, were thought to be designed as baby-making machines, freeing men from the burden of procreation and childbearing and allowing them the freedom to expend their energies in more noble and civilized pursuits, thereby implying that women were lower than men by the very nature and structure of the universe. One theory was that because women's procreative function was not needed in heaven, there was no need for women to have an immortal soul. William Acton, an English physician, advanced the argument that Nature provided the way to save men from the dangers of sex by making women more or less indifferent to sex (it was believed that unless the energy that went into sexual intercourse was carefully regulated, it could lead to nervous exhaustion). He was worried about the great drain on the nervous system caused by the loss of bodily fluids; he believed that the only solution was to engage in sex infrequently and then without prolonging the act. He suggested that this was possible because God had made women indifferent to sex deliberately to prevent the male's vital energy from being expended, and women acquiesced only out of fear of losing their husbands to prostitutes and ignored their natural distaste for the act in order to submit to their husbands.[2]

Chastity became the mark of gentility, and appearances counted more than reality. Bad women represented sexuality—good women stood for purity of mind and spirit. Creatively, women were restricted to certain areas. They could paint or sketch but not too creatively and not in oils. They could play an instrument but not professionally, and they could only play instruments that did not require spreading their legs, pursing their lips, viscerally demonstrating their muscles, or messing their dress or hairdo, which meant that they usually played the piano.

This citing of the physical female body in space leads to my examination of Taylor's *The Ticket-of-Leave Man*. The first act is set in the Bellevue Tea Gardens, a tavern adjacent to a concert room, in the suburbs of southwest London. The scene is crowded with waiters rushing about and patrons placing their orders. The main action of the play unfolds as villains Dalton and Moss set up naïve Lancashire lad Bob Brierly to take the fall for their counterfeiting scheme. Into this scene of controlled chaos and turmoil May Edwards enters with her guitar. She is confronted by the proprietor, Maltby, who tells her that he is "glad to see you're about again, but I can't have you cadging here." He grudgingly permits her to sing because she "was always a well-behaved girl, so, for once in a way—."[3] May sings her song but is rejected by the customers; not only do they jeer during her song, but they also refuse to tip her. After being similarly rejected by Brierly, May tells him, "I've not taken anything today, and I've not been well lately" (279). She then starts to faint and has to support herself with the back of a chair. Bob takes pity on her, gives her a glass of sherry to revive her, and loans her two sovereigns, telling her "take this, and stay thee quiet at home till thou'st i' fettle again" (283). Immediately following this exchange, Bob is arrested for passing counterfeit bills, ending the scene.

The first time we see May, we are told that she has not been well and that she is dependent on the benevolence of Maltby to let her sing in order to earn a pittance on which she presumably lives. Later in the scene we learn that she is "a helpless and friendless girl" who is "weak from the fever" and that she wishes for "some kind lady [who] would take me in. I'm quick at my needle; but who'd take me, a vagabond, without a friend to speak for me" (281). There are a number of issues at work in this opening scene. May finds herself in a public space, the object of a multifaceted gaze; she is not only observed by the theatre audience but also by Maltby, Bob Brierly, and the many different customers seated in the tavern. She desires to "be taken in by some kind lady," a desire that may be read in two ways. Not only does May wish to be sheltered, but she also literally wants to be taken in, to leave the public space and to work in a vocation that is socially acceptable to a

nineteenth-century audience. She has been ill, and we see that her un-
named malady is exacerbated by the fact that she is trying to make her
way in a public forum. Last, her instrument is a guitar. To reiterate two
of my earlier points: women could play an instrument but not professionally, which is exactly what May, in her own feeble way, is attempting
to do; and women were discouraged from playing an instrument that
demonstrated the use of their muscles. May plays the guitar, which is
physically placed in front of her, drawing attention to the area between
the breasts and genitalia, an area of the body inappropriate for general
viewing. In addition, the playing of a guitar requires that the arms are
held away from the musician, with definite and obvious use of muscu-
lature.

The second act takes place in May's room, in a boardinghouse. The
stage setting is described as follows:

> The room occupied by May Edwards in Mrs Willoughby's house, humbly
> but neatly furnished: flowers in the window, R. Flat; a work-table; stool;
> door communicating with her bedroom, R.; door leading to the staircase,
> L.; guitar hanging against wall; needlework on the table.
> May discovered with a birdcage on the table, arranging a piece of sugar
> and groundsel between the bars. (285)

We observe, by this description, how far May has progressed since the
first act, three years earlier. She has, in fact, been taken in by a kind
woman, as we see later when we meet Mrs. Willoughby. She is now in
the appropriate location for a working-class woman, in rooms "humbly
but neatly furnished, with flowers in the window." Her old nemesis, in
terms of social acceptability, the guitar, is now hanging on the wall,
almost literally shelved in terms of May's present life. Instead, we see
her new occupation foregrounded, her needlework arranged on the
table. We discover to what extent May has been domesticated in her
conversation with her bird:

> There, Goldie, I must give *you* your breakfast, though I don't care a bit
> for my own. Ah! You find singing a better trade than I did, you little
> rogue. I'm sure I shall have a letter from Robert this morning. I've all his
> letters here. . . . That's more than three years back. Oh! What an old
> woman I'm getting! It's no use denying it, Goldie. If you'll be quiet, like
> a good, well-bred canary, I'll read you Robert's last letter. (285)

May has rivaled Bob's enforced imprisonment with her own, socially
acceptable, caging. The parallels between her situation and Goldie's, the

canary's, are obvious. Goldie finds "singing a better trade" than May did; however, Goldie's singing takes place in the appropriate location, in the private sphere, in her gilded cage. May now also lives within the equivalent of a gilded cage and, like Goldie, is rewarded by Robert's letter for acting like a "good, well-bred canary."

This idea of a gilded cage is also seen in *The Drunkard*. The circumstances of Mary Wilson center almost entirely on her domestic setting. This temperance melodrama focuses on the trials and tribulations of Mary's husband, Edward Middleton, and his struggles with alcoholism; Mary exists in a separate sphere, acted on and commented on by the other characters but existing almost totally in isolation.

When the play begins, Mary and her mother, a recent widow, are threatened with eviction from their family home following the death of Edward's father. Old Mr. Middleton's wicked lawyer, Cribbs, is determined to force the women from their cottage, where they have lived for years. Cribbs attempts to sway Edward, now the landlord of the property, to his side, but Edward's decency comes through, and he will not be convinced: "Mr Cribbs, I cannot think of depriving them of a home, dear to them as the apple of their eyes—to send them forth from the flowers which they have reared, the vines which they have trained in their course—a place endeared to them by tender domestic recollections, and past remembrances of purity and religion."[4]

Mary, of course, has overheard the conversation, and declares her undying devotion and loyalty to Edward. Edward, who was smitten the moment he saw Mary, arranges to visit her in the cottage. The scene ends with Edward's lines: "Little did I think when I thought of selling that dear old cottage, that it should be regarded as a casket, invaluable for the jewel it contained." Again, we see the reinforcement of the domestic sphere that was prescribed for the ideal woman of the nineteenth century—within the home the woman is perceived as a commodity, a creature whose value is predicated on the approbation by her male counterpart. Mary's cottage is a perfect specimen for Edward's approval. It is described as a "pretty rural cottage . . . flowers, paintings, etc. Everything exhibits refined taste and elegant simplicity. Table, with bible and armchair, table and chair with embroidery frame" (252).

When Mary is first seen, the directions state that she is "seated by the table." There is no indication which table she is seated at; however, in her world it does not really matter. On one table is a Bible; at the other is an embroidery frame. Either site would be appropriate for a Victorian woman. This is the picture that Edward desires and one that Mary is dedicated to maintaining. She knows that a woman, without a man to provide a home as a safe haven, is constantly at risk of being cast out or compromised.

This last assertion is borne out when Edward's alcoholism takes over and he becomes a dissolute drunk, wandering the streets of New York. Mary and her daughter, Julia, have followed Edward to New York, apparently with the intention of finding Edward and bringing him home. Life in the city is inevitably more public; the description of their lodgings replicates the moral depravity that Edward's lifestyle has brought on the whole family: "A wretched garret. Old table and chair with lamp burning dimly. Mary in miserable apparel, sewing on slop-work; a wretched shawl thrown over her shoulders. Child sleeping on a straw bed on the floor, covered in part by a miserable ragged rug. Half a loaf of bread on the table. The ensemble of the scene indicates want and poverty" (284).

Although the text has already indicated that Edward's family has been reduced to these circumstances because of his drinking, there is no clear necessity for Mary and Julia to live in the abject indigence illustrated in this scene—after all, they still have the cottage, which is a freehold property, a legacy from Edward's father. I suggest that these characters demonstrate the Victorian effort to "make the home the centre of social life revolving around the family, paying great reverence to woman's role in raising children and in providing a haven for the male to retreat to from the outside world."[5] Because Edward's drinking led him away from the home, Mary felt compelled, as a good Victorian wife, to create a home, "a haven," near to where he actually was. Because Edward's alcoholism was clearly a social affliction, its effects were mirrored in the physical habitat and financial state of his family.

This idea is supported in the final act, after Edward has found salvation and a cure for his drinking in a local temperance society. The final scene is described as follows: "Interior of cottage as in Act 1st, Scene 1st. Everything denoting domestic peace and tranquil happiness. The sun is setting over the hills at back of landscape. Edward discovered near music stand. Julia seated on low stool. Mary sewing at handsome work table. Elegant table, with astral lamp, not lighted. Bible and other books on it. Two beautiful flower-stands, with roses, myrtles, etc., under window. Bird-cages on wings. Covers of tables, chairs, etc., all extremely neat, and in keeping" (302).

Everything about this scene indicates the restoration of domestic harmony. Not only has Edward stopped drinking, the family has returned to its rightful home. Mary is sewing, both in this scene and in the scene described previously; the difference is that she is sewing "slop-work" in her poverty-stricken locale, whereas she is working at a "handsome work table" after family peace has been reestablished. This is further exemplified by the fact that there is no dialogue in this scene but rather a musical interlude, with Edward accompanying Julia on the flute while she sings *Home, Sweet Home.*

Playwrights of nineteenth-century melodrama were quite clearly concerned with stage pictures and with specific roles assigned to women and men. "At the most fundamental level, particular constructions of 'womanness' defined the quality of being a 'man,' so that the natural identification of sexuality and desire with the feminine allowed the social and political construction of masculinity."[6] The Victorian patriarch in many ways required the presence of a woman not only as helpmate but also as a signifier of conformity to the ideal domestic situation. The attitude toward the Victorian family and family values as constructed by a patriarchal ideology was unyielding and, as illustrated by the examples from Taylor's *The Ticket-of-Leave Man* and Smith's *The Drunkard,* inextricably entrenched within the textual and scenographic dramaturgy of the nineteenth century.

Notes

1. Geoff Eley, "Nations, Publics, and Political Cultures: Placing Habermas in the Nineteenth Century," in *Habermas and the Public Sphere,* ed. Craig Calhoun (Cambridge, Mass.: MIT Press, 1992), 309.

2. Vern L. Bullough, *Sexual Variance in Society and History* (Chicago: University of Chicago Press, 1976), 544–45.

3. Tom Taylor, *The Ticket-of-Leave Man,* in *Nineteenth Century Plays,* ed. George Rowell (Oxford: Oxford University Press, 1972), 278. Subsequent quotations from this play are referenced parenthetically in the text.

4. William Henry Smith, *The Drunkard,* in *Early American Drama,* ed. Keffrey H. Richards (New York: Penguin, 1997), 255. Subsequent quotations from this play are referenced parenthetically in the text.

5. Bullough, *Sexual Variance,* 541.

6. Eley, "Nations," 309.

Seeing Double

Theatrical Strategy and
Cultural Anxieties in Boucicault

Brian T. Carney

DION BOUCICAULT (1820–90) HAS BEEN NOTED primarily for his remarkable ability to appeal to large and diverse audiences. As Oscar Brockett notes, Boucicault's appeal is generally credited to his "sentimentality, wit, sensationalism and local color."[1] Although these elements are certainly present in all of his plays, a closer examination of one of his most successful works—*The Colleen Bawn* (1860)—offers a more subtle explanation for his success: his ability to adapt the structure and vision of the traditional melodrama to the needs of the emergent business class. By doubling his characters, especially his heroines, and splitting his narrative focus between paired characters on different sides of major social divides, Boucicault was able to offer a model for respectable behavior and proper relations between and among social classes.[2]

In *Melodrama Unveiled: American Theatre and Culture, 1800–1850,* David Grimsted outlines the structure and vision of the traditional melodrama that served as the basis for Boucicault's innovations. Grimsted describes melodramas as indistinguishable plays of undeviating character, purpose, and purity. The most important element of the plays is Virtue and its personification, particularly in the heroine, whose outer beauty is the sign of even greater inner beauty. Because of this Virtue, she does not have a sense of humor, and she is neither the author nor the subject of humorous remarks. She excels at passive values such as modesty, patience, and meekness and must be protected from external hazards, especially sexual threats, as well as from her own weakness. The external threat is provided by the villain, whose evil behavior is generally unmotivated but who always has one fair goal—the heroine. Her protection is provided by the hero, who is generally a perfect shield for the heroine's virtue. Finally, a wise old father offers good advice and reminds the heroine to protect her purity.[3]

Beyond these four central characters, standard melodramas also featured low-comedy characters, generally lower-class men and women who provided what little comic relief was offered and who were generally not integrated into the main plot. The low-comedy woman, or "lively girl," generally mocked stage conventions and conventional pieties, although she did so from within strict parameters. The low-comedy man presented a sectional or national type such as the sharp-dealing Yankee, the English farmer, the quaint Irishman, the happy misspeaking Negro, the noble-but-somewhat-suspect Indian, or the urban gallant (Grimsted, 183–92). These stock characters, according to Grimsted, were placed into a plot whose "threads formed a Gordian knot of ridiculous complexity which the dramatist finally cut by near miracle" and whose structure "was seldom thoughtfully worked out" (234). These situations also upheld a strict social structure while paying lip service to democratic ideals and allowing some flexibility for natural nobility and for love as the great potential social equalizer. Above all, argues Grimsted, the cornerstone of society was domestic happiness, which was brought about by female purity (196–234).

Bruce McConachie demonstrates, however, in *Melodramatic Formations: American Theatre and Society, 1820–1870*, that by the mid-nineteenth century traditional melodrama's unbreakable link between self-control and economic success no longer matched the experience and needs of the emergent business class. Because men could lose their economic standing through the vagaries of the marketplace through no fault of their own, new definitions of respectability had to be developed and disseminated.[4] A new social order had to be constructed based on one's "natural" abilities resulting from birth and upbringing rather than on inner qualities of character and morality or historical contingencies of wealth or traditional social position (McConachie, 215–17). Creating this new social structure necessitated redefining the behavior of and relations between the classes and the sexes. The working class was divided between the respectable, who espoused middle-class values, and the naturally dependent, who did not. Women were no longer the passive focus of domestic happiness but its ferocious defenders when the need arose. Men were caught between the sincerity and repression of parlor life and the ruthless rationality of the business world. To alleviate this tension, men were allowed to use social masks to hide their true nature and to offer sincere repentance if their masks ever slipped too far (McConachie, 219–22). By facilitating these changes, the emergent business class was able to cement its cultural hegemony.

McConachie further contends that these cultural shifts required additional alterations in the construction of the melodramatic spectacles that were so popular with both upper and lower classes. The structure of traditional melodramas relied on the causal links between moral behavior (or the lack thereof) and its reward (or punishment). However, with an increased emphasis on happenstance, villains were placed in a more benign role, and someone had to determine which events were brought by chance and which by human agency. Because the new hero was too conflicted to define himself, let alone determine causality, the character of the detective emerged to uncover the truth (McConachie, 223).

Boucicault's move away from traditional melodrama and toward business-class melodrama is perhaps best seen in *The Colleen Bawn,* which centers on the romantic and economic travails of the lower-class Eily O'Connor (the Colleen Bawn, or fair-haired lass) and the upper-class Anne Chute (the Colleen Ruadh, or red-haired lass), who ultimately become allies in their pursuit of marriage and material happiness. However, the play also includes several other pairs of doubled characters.

A brief summary is in order here: Eily is secretly married to Hardress Cregan, impoverished upper-class owner of a Killarney estate. The marriage is secret because Hardress is ashamed of Eily's lower-class manners and speech and because his mother expects him to marry the wealthy Anne to save the estate. Anne is in love with Kyrle Daly, a college friend of Cregan's, but their romance is thwarted when Danny, Cregan's crippled boatman, tricks her into thinking Kyrle is in love with Eily. To further protect Hardress, Danny has pledged to kill Eily if Hardress gives him his glove. Hardress orders Danny not to harm Eily, but his mother later gives Danny the glove. Anne visits Eily to discover the truth of her relationship with Kyrle, but she misunderstands Eily's confessions and gets lost on her way home. Myles-Na-Coppaleen, a roguish peasant who is also in love with Eily, rescues Anne as Danny leads Eily to a water cave, where he intends to drown her. Myles saves Eily and wounds Danny, whose sickbed confession is overheard by the scoundrel Squire Corrigan, who lusts after both Mrs. Cregan and the estate. As Anne is about to marry Hardress, Corrigan bursts in to arrest Cregan for Eily's murder, but everything is set right when wise Father Tom produces Eily, and both couples are happily and richly reunited.

By centering his complicated narrative on the interwoven plights of the two heroines and doubling other characters as well, Boucicault was able to close the gap between the strictures of traditional melodramatic structure and the changing needs of his audiences. For example, he turns the single passive heroine of traditional melodrama into two spirited heroines whose apparent differences are smoothed over and who also merge the features of the heroine and the "lively girl." From the subtitle of the play *(The Brides of Garryowen)* to their linked appellations, their stories are cleverly and completely interwoven. Their deep connection even structures the action of the play. In the first scene they are mistakenly established as rivals for both Hardress and Kyrle, a mistake that sets the plot in motion. After they pledge friendship in act 2, their bond is underscored in the ensuing scenes where Myles rescues Anne from the storm as Danny takes Eily to her apparent doom, from which Myles then rescues her. And in act 3 they are ultimately able to bridge the social tensions that threatened to divide them.

Further, Anne and Eily do share one important characteristic with the traditional heroine of melodrama: their essential goodness is unquestioned throughout the play, a point that Boucicault stresses and that remains an important part of the social code being established by the business class. In a lovely song Myles says Eily is worth any amount of worldly riches.

Further, Danny's mother, Sheelah, praises Eily for the purity and steadfastness of her love, proclaims that all of nature recognizes the beauty of her voice, and offers her blessings on the tangled romance between Eily and Hardress. Even Danny, whose devotion to Hardress outweighs his affection for Eily, praises her extravagantly: "The looking-glass was never made that could do her justice; and if St. Patrick wanted a wife, where would he find an angel that 'ud compare with the Colleen Bawn. As I row her on the lake, the little fishes come up to look at her; and the wind from heaven lifts up her hair to see what the devil brings her down here at all."[5]

Throughout the play Anne is praised less fulsomely than Eily because her social standing and money, as well as her graces, are sufficient markers of her proper business-class values. However, Myles still cannot resist praising her: "Sure there isn't a boy in the County Kerry that would not give two thumbs off his hands to do a service to the Colleen Ruadh, as you are called among us. Ah! Then it's the purty girl she is in them long clothes" (*CB*, 82).

Eily's only shortcomings are her lack of money and her failure to speak well, the markers of a social status at odds with her natural excellence and the barriers to acknowledging her marriage to Cregan. A distraught Cregan discusses this fact with Danny, and later he shouts at Eily for not speaking properly.

Unlike the traditional melodramatic heroine, however, neither of the Colleens is a passive victim of villainy or circumstance. Both actively pursue what they want. Eily has flown in the face of society by marrying the upper-class Hardress, and although she tries to please him by using proper language, she still vigorously defends her old friends to him. She decides to leave Hardress, so he can marry Anne, and to build a new life for herself. Anne actively pursues both Kyrle and Hardress. Immediately following her first entrance, she starts flirting with Kyrle. When she discovers what she thinks is his relationship with Eily, she does not take it quietly but taunts Kyrle with her knowledge, and when she discovers his apparent marriage to Eily, she proposes to Hardress.

Finally, from their first meeting to the final lines of the play, the two heroines are friends despite their apparent rivalry and their different social status. They even manage to blur the most important markers of social distinction in the play: money and language. When Anne swears Eily and Danny to secrecy about her visit, she accepts Eily's word as a lady, but she offers Danny money to ensure his silence. By paying the mortgage on the Cregan estate, Anne restores Hardress and raises Eily to the economic standing that should accompany their social standing. Anne also removes language as a barrier between them. During her first flight with Kyrle, she slips unapologetically into a brogue: "Well, I can't help it. When I am angry the brogue comes out, and my Irish heart will burst through manners, and graces, and twenty stay-laces. I'll give up my fortune, I will" (*CB*, 72–73). Anne's ability to slip into a brogue offsets Eily's inability to speak properly. In the final lines of the play Anne reassures Eily that her speech is fine and that they will always be friends.

Although it is easy to see the active and cooperative women as the heroines of the play, it is more difficult to see the passive Hardress and Kyrle as heroes. Perhaps it is more accurate to refer to their roles as husbands given that their narrative significance comes largely from their status as beloveds of the women. Hardress was unable to resist a secret marriage to Eily and was then unable to figure a way out of his dilemma, and in his confusion he resorts to shouting and cruelty. This behavior contrasts sharply with the unwavering and unselfish devotion of Myles to Eily and of Danny to Hardress. Likewise, Kyrle is unable to help his friend or figure out the confusion that nearly destroys his relationship with Anne. Neither Myles nor Danny thinks of searching for the missing Eily nor takes any action to resolve the mystery. This is somewhat ameliorated by their youth; at several points in the play Boucicault highlights the fact that they are in their late twenties. Further, both men are very sensitive to language as a class barrier—Hardress insisting that Eily learn to speak properly and Kyrle shocked at Anne's slipping into brogue. Although neither man has an apparent profession or source of income, each insists on and observes all the prerogatives and rites of class. Only by following the examples of their intendeds are they able to overcome their social paralysis.

The villains of the play are clearly marked, yet they are also clearly differentiated from their traditional melodramatic roles. Both are given clear motivations and are interested in the aristocratic Cregans rather than the heroines. Squire Corrigan has been in love with Mrs. Cregan for fifteen years and is willing to forgive the debt if she will marry him. Only when his love is thwarted and mocked by Hardress does he take definite action against the family—foreclosing on the mortgage and arresting Hardress for the murder of Eily. His foolishness—as opposed to his villainy—is punished lightly by a dunking in the horse pond.

Danny, on the other hand, is a more serious villain. His devotion to Hardress is so total that he tries to kill Eily, reasoning that if she was as devoted to Hardress as he was, she would gladly die for his sake. He pays for this villainy with his life. However, the audience's reaction to Danny is mollified by his role as Hardress's shadow, an evil double who becomes the scapegoat for Hardress's weaknesses.

Unlike traditional melodrama *The Colleen Bawn* does not include a wise father figure because the declining paternalistic hegemony is unable to provide any advice for the emergent business class. Boucicault, however, divides the function of adviser between the two additional pairs of characters. The play features two mothers who are fiercely protective of their sons. Even though Mrs. Cregan and Sheelah are on different sides of the class divide, they use similar language in the defense of their erring children. When she is taken to Castle Chute to testify about Danny's confession, Sheelah denounces Corrigan; "Divil a word—it's lie from end to end, that ould thief was niver in my cabin—he invented the whole of it—sure you're the divil's own parverter of the truth!" (*CB*, 101). Mrs. Cregan takes a similar tone when Corrigan arrives to arrest Hardress: "I am his mother—the hunters are after my blood!" (*CB*, 98–99).

Further, both women attest to Eily's goodness and rightful place as Hardress's bride. For Sheelah, who acts as a servant to Eily even though they are of the same social class, Eily's right to marry Hardress is never questioned, and she speaks admiringly of Eily's great devotion in the face of adversity. Recognizing that Eily's natural goodness effectively raises her to a higher social class and then treating her appropriately, Sheelah serves as a role model for the lower class. Mrs. Hardress initially disapproves of Eily but offers her approval—and her apologies—when Eily returns with Father Tom.

In addition an odd pair serves as foster parents to Eily—Father Tom and Myles. When Father Tom discovers Eily hiding in Myles's cottage, both men claim rights of parentage:

> FATHER TOM: Eily, you have but one home, and that's my poor house. You are not alone in the world—there's one beside ye, your father, and that's myself.
> MYLES: Two-bad luck to me, two. I am her mother; sure I brought her into the world a second time. (*CB*, 94)

Throughout the play Myles's service to both Anne and Eily helps smooth over class differences and serves as a model for proper relations between the classes. His deference to the ladies and his defiance of inconvenient restrictions on his business also offer a model for business-class behavior. And Father Tom, in his relaxed attitude toward whiskey punch and tobacco, as well as the marriage of Eily and Hardress, as opposed to Hardress's priggishness on both issues, also serves as a model of natural morality and class relations. He is also the detective in the play, searching for the information necessary to publicly unite Eily and Hardress.

Finally, Boucicault uses humor to make sure all class divisions are smoothed over. Unlike their predecessors both Anne and Eily are witty and charming. Eily sings "Cruiskeen Lawn" and "Pretty Girl Milking Her Cow," comic songs that underscore her ultimate pride in her peasant roots. In both her flirtation with and abuse of Kyrle Anne is also quite witty, and her descriptions of Kyrle ("his heart can be no trifle if he's all in proportion") and Corrigan ("a potato on a silver plate") serve to define them in their structural and thematic roles of deserving husband and pretentious villain (*CB*, 53).

By doubling the characters and functions of traditional melodrama, especially with closely linked heroines of different classes, and by altering the forces that shape the narrative, Boucicault is able to yoke the reigning melodramatic paradigm to the service of the emergent business class's hegemony. More specifically, Boucicault is able to smooth over these cultural anxieties by creating what Fredric Jameson has called an *ideologeme*. In brief, Jameson describes an ideologeme as the minimal unit of a larger class discourse that rewrites and restores a class horizon and that mediates between conceptions of ideology as abstract opinion, class value, and the like and narrative materials. This formation can be read simultaneously as a conceptual description or as a narrative manifestation, taking the appearance of either a philosophical system or a cultural text.[6] In the case of *The Colleen Bawn* and his other melodramas, Boucicault's reconstruction of the melodramatic paradigm serves as both a model for relations within and between the classes and genders and as an engrossing theatrical narrative.

Boucicault was able to replicate this dramatic ideologeme by reconfiguring the mythemes that make up his narrative. According to Claude Lévi-Strauss myth functions as a dialectic, first presenting material as a binary then resolving the tension inherent in that dualism by the use of a mediating third term. Mythemes are the smallest units of this breakdown, and they are continually reconfigured into new mythological narratives.[7]

Traditional melodrama relied on the tensions inherent in such binary social markers as good and evil, upper class and lower class, male and female, hero and villain. Each character and each narrative element was trapped in these rigid dualisms, which served to reinforce the cultural hegemony of the paternalistic elite of the early 1800s. Instead of insisting on these strict categories of behavior, Boucicault blurred these distinctions by doubling his characters. By bridging the differences between characters on opposing sides of various social divides, Boucicault was able to create the necessary illusion of unified support for the emerging hegemony of the business class and to help define proper relationships within the new structures. Thus, the upper-class Anne and the lower-class Eily become friends and allies, and the roguish peasant Myles gladly works to support them. Villainous plots and social markers behind them, and beaming peasants beside them, the Colleen Bawn and the Colleen Ruadh happily begin their married lives as the best of friends.

With these complex webs of doubling, Boucicault has moved his melodrama far away from the traditional paradigm. He has replaced a pallid heroine with two active and witty heroines, the unwavering hero with a man of commerce torn between his duty and his feelings, and the monochromatic villain with a more nuanced figure who can serve as society's scapegoat. Boucicault has also replaced the wise father figure with a comic successor because the young Turks of the emergent business class could not rely on the standards of the waning paternalistic elite. These new characters and structures supported the requirements of the hegemony of the new business class—the need to decouple self-control and economic success, the need to separate happenstance and human agency, the need for men to wear social masks in the boardroom and the parlor, the need for women to defend their homes—when necessary and the need of the lower class to uphold the values of the business class. Boucicault was able to do this by cleverly doubling his characters, providing everyone in his audience with someone to cheer for and with a surrogate who showed them the way to behave properly by the new business-class standards. The secret to Boucicault's success was his ability to closely match the social needs and desires of his audiences; perhaps the closeness of that match was the reason for his later lowered standing as the author of "sentimentality, wit, sensationalism and local color."[8]

Notes

1. Oscar G. Brockett, *History of the Theatre,* 4th ed. (Boston: Allyn and Bacon, 1982).

2. Dion Boucicault, *The Colleen Bawn* (1860), in *The Dolmen Boucicault,* ed. David Krause (Chester Springs, Pa.: Dufour Editions, 1963). For other examples of this doubling see Dion Boucicault, *The Corsican Brothers* (1852), in *Three Early Potboilers,* vol. 4 of *Dion Boucicault, the Shaughraun,* ed. Sven Eric Molin and Robin Goodfellow (N.p.: Proscenium Press, 1989); ibid., *The Octoroon* (1859) and *The Shaughraun* (1874), in *Plays by Dion Boucicault,* ed. Peter Thomson (Cambridge: Cambridge University Press, 1984); and ibid., *The Poor of New York,* in *American Melodrama,* ed. Daniel C. Gerould (New York: Performing Arts Journal Publications, 1983).

3. David Grimsted, *Melodrama Unveiled: American Theatre and Culture, 1800–1850* (Chicago: University of Chicago Press, 1968). Subsequent quotations from this source are referenced parenthetically in the text.

4. Bruce McConachie, *Melodramatic Functions: American Theatre and Society, 1820–1870* (Iowa City: University of Iowa Press, 1992). Subsequent quotations from this source are referenced parenthetically in the text.

5. Boucicault, *The Colleen Bawn,* 57. Subsequent quotations from this source are referenced parenthetically in the text with the abbreviation *CB.*

6. Fredric Jameson, *The Political Unconscious: Narrative as a Socially Symbolic Act* (Ithaca, N.Y.: Cornell University Press, 1981).

7. Claude Lévi-Strauss, *Myth and Meaning* (New York: Schocken, 1979).

8. Brockett, *History of the Theatre.*

Part II: Cross-Dressing,

Commodity, and Community

The Stage Is Not the Place

for Real Women

The Odd Career of Lulu Glaser

Martha S. LoMonaco

THE NAME "LULU GLASER" WAS a household word in turn-of-the-century America. Glaser was the reigning queen of the comic opera stage, one of the most popular and lucrative entertainments of the late nineteenth century. Although by 1900 the public was beginning to tire of these formulaic, frothy musicals, Glaser kept both herself and the form alive through her lively character portrayals of the ideal American girl—pretty, dainty, vivacious, pert yet sufficiently modest in demeanor, and, most especially, young. Unwilling and unable to reinvent herself, Glaser retired in 1917 at the age of forty-three "with no regrets," having declared as early as 1907 that, "the stage is not the place for real women because actresses do not live; they just exist."[1]

Glaser's life and career exemplify the totality of turn-of-the-century American women. She was concurrently one of the pioneer professional women, supporting herself via a career, and a popular representative, both on- and offstage, of the celebrated domestic woman, heralded as mainstay of home and family. These are clearly contradictory positions, exacerbated by the illusory world of the stage. The notion of a workingwoman was anathema to the general public unless a woman had neither husband nor father to provide support. Glaser's stage persona was a glamorized version of this dependent creature who may be

Lulu Glaser. Lulu Glaser Papers, Theatre Collection Visual Materials Division, Department of Rare Books and Special Collections, Princeton University Library. Used by permission.

clever and spirited but, ultimately, becomes the hero's adoring wife. The irony, of course, is that an actress needed to work in order to portray these ideal ladies. Glaser's fascination lies in a series of conflicting needs and desires. She methodically set about building a career but really wanted to stay at home and—although a role model for professional women—frequently proclaimed that a woman's real job was as wife and mother. Simultaneously, Glaser was the enchanting performer, the ruthless businesswoman who managed her own company for twelve years, a fashion trendsetter and icon of American femininity who smiled sweetly from the covers of ladies' magazines and popular sheet music, the bearer of a license to carry a gun, and an advocate for women staying at home. One could say that she was both a product and a victim of her time.

While growing up outside of Pittsburgh, Pennsylvania, in the 1880s Glaser was an aspiring singer and devotee of all things theatrical. Her early diaries detail performances attended (194 as of 1890), performers admired, and her own aspirations to join their ranks. Her wish came true in November 1891 when Francis Wilson engaged her as a chorus member in his popular opera troupe. Within six months she had become a principal soubrette and by 1895 company prima donna. In her final season with Wilson, 1899–1900, she shared star billing before breaking out on her own the following year with the Lulu Glaser Opera Company.

By the time she left Wilson, Glaser had developed the charismatic stage persona that reached its apotheosis in *Dolly Varden*. This 1901 comic opera by Julian Edwards and Stanislaus Strange, written expressly to accentuate Glaser's talents, incited a nationwide love affair with Dolly during the show's three-year tour. It became her biggest hit and the only show for which she was long remembered largely because it mellifluously combined Glaser's talents with the public's desire for froth and fancy. The show also seems to have had a better book than most comic operas; as one critic put it, "it is a comic opera with the accent strong on 'comic' and a secondary one on 'opera.' "[2]

Dolly Varden is set in 1730 and is the story of an innocent country girl brought to the city by a guardian who has designs on both her hand and her sizable fortune. His greatest fear is that she will fall in love and run off with one of her many admirers; thus, he fabricates ingenious plans to prevent the worst from happening. For instance, when Dolly goes out for her daily exercise, he makes her trot along inside a sedan chair from which the flooring has been removed. Thus, on her first entrance Dolly is almost completely screened from view except for her feet and ankles. In the early twentieth century this was considered an alluring sight, indeed, and "I Love My Dolly's Ankles and Feet" became one of the show's most popular numbers.

In its long run from 1901–4 *Dolly Varden* became not only the most sought-after theatre ticket but a source of emulation in music and especially in fashion. The opera capitalized on the magnificent European court fashions of the 1730s. The same styles had enjoyed a notable revival in the 1860s and thus were being repopularized by Glaser. She contended that "the correct idea of Dolly Varden conveys a suggestion of pink June roses, pea-blossoms, pretty gardens with greensward and a sweet, dainty maiden."[3] Her gowns, hats, white silk mitts and pink slippers were soon copied and distributed nationwide by leading New York fashion houses. There was a plethora of "Dolly Varden" teas, garden parties, and cotillions that would feature "I Love My Dolly's Ankles and Feet." As the music played, the ladies would show off their fanciful ankle-length dresses modeled directly after Glaser's costumes. It is no wonder that throughout the rest of her career she was often referred to as "Dolly."[4]

Glaser, ever the astute businesswoman, created a demand for Dolly that concurrently became a demand for Glaser. Her characterization was grounded in the classic stage soubrette that she had perfected under Wilson—saucy, bubbling, boisterous, what was popularly known as a hoyden—to which Glaser added the more delicate sensibilities appropriate for a leading lady. Youth, boundless energy, and a well-proportioned slender figure were essential ingredients, as was Glaser's distinctive gurgling giggle, which became her trademark. She appealed to both sexes, with women seeking to emulate her clothes and manners and men desiring merely a stage glance in their direction. An anonymous verse summed up her attractions:

> Lulu, dancing lightly,
> Lulu, laughing brightly,
> Lulu, singing sprightly,
> Your glances haunt me yet.
> I think 'twas last December
> I saw you—or November—
> The piece I can't remember
> But *you* I can't forget.[5]

It is one thing to create such a character while young; it is quite another to sustain this character over a number of years, particularly if, like Glaser's Dolly, the character is so dependent on the vitality and good looks of youth. Many performers of the period developed self-identifying stage personas—Joseph Jefferson with Rip Van Winkle, James O'Neill with the Count of Monte Cristo, and Lillian Russell with the "American Beauty"—but all found ways to sustain or adapt them with the changing times and their own advancing age. Also, the best of these actors had multiple talents that either ameliorated or substituted for the loss of beauty and vigor. Men have always been more successful at playing romantic heroes well past their prime; women, conversely, have had to be extremely clever and versatile performers to preserve careers as their faces wrinkled, figures filled out, and hair grayed. Russell managed to do this as did other notable actresses of the period, including Ada Rehan, Maude Adams, and Minnie Maddern

Fiske. But Glaser, like Jefferson and O'Neill, embodied a public figure inseparable from the stage persona. Subject to the classic double standard, Glaser's Dolly faded, whereas the men's characters aged gracefully. Jefferson and O'Neill both performed well into their seventies, but Glaser was finished at forty-three.

Diminishing beauty and the onset of middle age were not the only obstacles she encountered in trying to maintain her career. Equally detrimental was what was clearly a limited range of talents. Glaser created her popular stage personas largely out of youthful energy and charisma rather than from carefully honed, individualized characterizations. For nearly twenty years critics described all of her performances using the same narrow set of adjectives: *bubbling, vivacious, tireless, spirited.* She was never considered a great singer, and by the time she was touring in *Mlle. Mischief,* her last major success, many critics began to point out other shortcomings as well. One critic averred that, like her mentor, Francis Wilson, Glaser's comedy was dependent on her charm and "a box full of tricks" rather than on "the impersonation of a laughable character."[6] Percy Hammond, of the *Chicago Post,* concurred, stating that her appeal "is rather in what she is than in what she does."[7] But both critics admitted that audiences really didn't seem to mind because they continued to be enamored by her funny walk and distinctive laugh. That walk is characterized in the *Chicago Record Herald* as a "method of hoop-la." The writer explained that in the previous evening's performance "she bounded hilariously from chair to table, instantly changed her mind and landed on the floor. She defined with a hop, skip and a jump the various moods that possessed her."[8] A critic for the *Chicago Journal* described the same performance as "full of the divvyl," and he equated Glaser with a "jumping jack" who has "never been more energetic."[9] Her accompanying laugh, reported as everything from an "assiduous chirp" to a "deep-throated gurgle," was praised in the *Detroit Journal* as "an exhilaration, a tonic, an intoxicant," and the *Boston Traveler* suggested that Glaser should "copyright and phonograph" it because "it's her one best asset."[10]

Glaser's unwillingness to persevere had as much to do with her professional disenchantment as it did with her decidedly limited talents and the vicissitudes of an aging body. Thanks to Francis Wilson's support and careful mentoring, she became the star she had dreamed of as a child. The glamour diminished quickly, however, once she was out on her own and saddled with the difficulties of managing both career and company. She lamented her predicament in an essay written circa 1907:

The stage is not the place for real women because actresses do not live; they just exist. And they exist on that very ephemeral and quite unsatisfying diet—public approval and popular admiration. If actresses even get a glimpse of real life, if they ever have the opportunity to get a wee taste of the joys of sincerity in living, it is because they have sense enough to slip away from their artificial stage existence for a short while, and take a good, deep, pure breath of freedom on the outside. ("Home")

Her essay, found among press releases and publicity items in her archives now housed at Princeton University, seems intended for publication, particularly because Glaser concludes by voicing doubts that her words will be taken seriously. "I can hear," she laments, "numbers of those who read this, remark: 'She doesn't mean it. She is just posing. She just wants to cause a little more talk and get a little more advertising.' "

Not surprisingly, there is no evidence that the essay ever made it into print. It is far too frank—even hostile—in its views of an unfeeling public and the unglamorous portrayal of the actor's life on the road. "Fame and glory and popular admiration are mockeries," she contends, blaming "the constant, nagging, undercurrent spirit of criticism rampant in the audiences, in the reading public, even in our own ranks" for her unease. Glaser defies a public unwilling to appreciate the hardships of life on tour with its ill-smelling train berths and windowless, filthy dressing rooms, but all too eager to condemn and judge her frailties: "The star cannot, must not, shall not, dare not, be human enough to have the slightest thing the matter with us. If she does dare to commit this act of treason, only death is considered cause enough to relieve her from the necessity of coming out on the stage, smirking and smiling into the bright glare of the footlights at an audience that hasn't the slightest appreciation of her self sacrifice" ("Home").

Despite her unhappiness, she admits that the public generally has been good to her and that she has "gained a measure of pleasure" from her work. Ultimately, however, the greatest reward of the profession seems to be the ability to make sufficient money so that one can "quit the gilded mockery for the real home." "A woman should be a wife and mother," Glaser proudly contends, for "she will not find genuine happiness in any other sphere" ("Home").

Glaser's essay can be viewed as stating the frustrations of a performer anxious for a worthy successor to *Dolly Varden* (the tour ended in 1904) and as a newlywed (Glaser married costar Ralph Herz during her 1906 tour of *Miss Dolly Dollars*) who, perhaps, is having second thoughts about her life and career. Was she contemplating retirement, and possibly settling down to the domestic bliss she advocates here? Was she fed up with a profession she did not love and for which, psychologically, she was ill suited? Was she really in it for the money and the promise of future security? She longs for retirement and vows that "when I do retire, I shall retire." "The most pathetic thing," she asserts, "is to see an actress, once the popular idol of our great country, return to the stage and receive not fresh laurels but a bunch of dried leaves—the ashes of past triumphs" ("Home"). Whatever she contemplated, she would continue to work steadily for the next ten years in a career she may not have loved but that had proven steady and lucrative.

The years under Francis Wilson's tutelage developed her not only as a performer but also as a businessperson and collector of books, fine art, and autographed letters. Unlike other stage performers, Glaser, alongside her mentor, invested her earnings carefully and devoted free afternoons on tour to scouring local shops in search of valuable treasures at bargain prices. She also invested in real estate and owned homes in Pennsylvania, New York, and Connecticut to which she retreated as often as possible—often to the detriment of her company—to rest and surround herself with the things she loved.

As Wilson groomed the star performer and collector, he concurrently created a woman capable of leading her own company. He advised her on all aspects of management, from the psychology of handling people to the difficulties of handling finances. He warned her against using her own money to finance productions. "You will find plenty of managers who will pay you a certain salary per week and a percentage of the receipts beside," he assured her. It is also apparent that he understood her all too well and could predict where problems might arise; as such, he presented his concerns tenderly. "The cares of employing a company and attending to a *million* things when the company is your very own, would be interesting at the start," he advised, "but very wearing and *aging* speedily after, to a woman of your nervous temperament." He further warned that "the worry of providing new material is appalling and should never fall upon you."[11]

Although Wilson's advice was sound and Glaser seemed inclined to follow it, things did not work out as expected. She did hire a manager, a rapid succession of them, in fact—the list boasted some of the most famous names in show business, including Charles Dillingham, Abe Erlanger, and Lee and J. J. Shubert—but found none satisfactory beyond a few seasons. She tried not to invest her own funds but found herself bankrolling several of her companies. And the dearth of suitable material was a constant worry that largely fell on her. Comic opera was a rapidly dying form, and the musical comedies both she and Wilson could have counted on to further their careers were still several decades away.

As the years passed and the search for better vehicles and managements became a growing frustration, Glaser gained a reputation for being difficult. It is hard to ascertain how much of this reputation was warranted by her behavior, how much was the delight of gossip-hungry journalists eager for controversy, and how much was antifeminist rant. Presumably, all three combined to paint an unflattering portrait when her interests and power were in direct confrontation with what was then, and is still, a male-dominated industry. As early as the end of her first full season, the press was already casting a dour light on her double role as performer and businesswoman. In an unidentified clipping dated June 22, 1901, the headline blared, "Lulu Glaser, a Woman of Contrasts." The article continues: "Miss Glaser is the only soubrette alive who takes life seriously. She is apparently the giddiest and breeziest thing possible in the footlights' glare, but off the stage she is about as plain, matter-of-fact, and businesslike a proposition as managers have to do with. Miss Glaser and A. H. Chamberlyn have ceased business relations, and she will be managed next season by Fred C. Whitney, though she is eminently capable of performing that office herself."[12]

Whitney managed the full three-year tour of *Dolly Varden* but not without incident or a sharp exchange of words. While the company was touring Canada in January 1902, Whitney was laid up with an injury in upstate New York and Glaser took charge. As one newspaper put it, "in the absence of the manager she believes the star should be the commander-in-chief, and conducts herself as such." When her advance agent, John McKinney, got out of line, she was forced to "introduce corporeal punishment into the curriculum in the interests of discipline." Interestingly, the papers fail to relate what he did to raise her ire, but they happily detail her punishment of boxing his ears. "It is said that the small and shapely hands of the very agile singer descended upon his ears with such amazing rapidity that McKinney was the best boxed man in the King's Dominions before he had the time to gather his scattered senses." Although McKinney was set to demand an apology once Whitney was back at the helm, "the pugnacious little woman is authority for the statement that none will be forthcoming. Discipline, she avers, must and shall be preserved in the *Dolly Varden* company."[13]

Whitney would sue her for breach of contract in 1904 when, finally fed up with his management, she left him for Charles Dillingham. Although the tour was a success, Whitney's management style cost Glaser her health and well-being by forcing a long succession of one-night stands. She complained of these stresses in December 1902, detailing her illnesses in a six-page letter and asking him to please discuss matters with her in person. Although her tone is businesslike, it is also reasonable. "I want to arrange this matter pleasantly and will try to do so if you will come here," she writes. "If we cannot, I then insist on all my rights under the contract, and demand that you immediately send me all the box office statements which you have failed to give me, and to pay over to me what is coming to me, under the contract, and if you wish to cancel the contract you may do so at once." She complains of being a nervous wreck and relates her distress at having to take on her shoulders "much of the work of the Company which I was not called upon to do."[14] Even if she abrogated some financial control to her managers, it is clear that Glaser always maintained total artistic control of her productions. Managers would make suggestions but were always careful to couch their ideas in a nonthreatening tone. Charles Dillingham, in a 1906 letter written during the *Miss Dolly Dollars* tour, nervously responded to her suggestions for improving the show before playing Chicago. "It is alright to take the horse out," he tells her, "but if I were you I would put it in for Chicago, especially the first night, but if it worries you don't do it, I mean it is up to you."[15] In her greatest artistic triumph, *Dolly Varden,* she happily took credit not only for her winning character portrayal but for the totality of the operetta. She believed that via *Dolly* she personally had reformed all operettas from crude, slapstick farces to wholesome family entertainments. As she told one reporter:

> Have you noticed the absence of the clown comedian? That was another thing I made up my mind to dispense with. No more buffoonery. It sickened me. No more horse play, slapping one another over and walking around the stage on bow legs with a make-up that would give one nausea. I am not making a bold attempt to uplift the stage; do not misunderstand me; but I do mean to put it on a wholesome level as far as I am personally concerned.[16]

Her insistence that "the clown comedian is dead to me" could be viewed as a rather unkind recrimination of the very character popularized by her mentor, Francis Wilson. It is more likely, however, simply an attempt to attract a wider audience to her new operetta, which was indeed different from its predecessors. The principal innovation was in the character of Dolly herself, which maintained enough of the verve of a soubrette to make her interesting but was imbued with a delicacy that seemed to many observers the "best type of American girl on the comic opera stage today." Glaser and Dolly were one in the eyes and ears of the public, embodying "the frankness and dash which all true Americans expect to find in a young and beautiful woman of their own nationality." Yet her portrayal was not so frank as to defy the girlishness that her audiences so admired. Rather, she "transcended the mannishness" of the "kicking soubrette" in favor of "a certain daintiness and delicacy, sufficiently refined to fit in harmonious relation to the pretty framework of the opera."[17] Glaser realized quickly the market value of Dolly and did her best to remind the public that the Dolly/Lulu hybrid was, indeed, the apotheosis of the ideal American girl. As she told one interviewer: "I must tell you that Dolly Varden is the first character I have ever played that suited me. How I love her! I never before felt as I do about Dolly. I play with her as a girl would with a doll. I am never so happy as when I am Dolly Varden."[18]

The transformation of Glaser to Dolly extended even into those arenas that made Glaser stand apart—for instance, in her book collecting. Glaser's mother, who doubled as official chaperone, gleefully informed a reporter that she had returned to New York to dust her daughter's two-thousand-volume library: "You see, books are Loo-loo's one fad and she allows no one but me to handle them." She quickly relegates the books to the level of play things, however, as she relates how "Loo-loo" walks into her library to greet—not read—her collection: " 'How do you do?' she says out loud to her books and then she goes up to her piano and opens it and says 'how do you do?' to it."[19]

Despite a second Dolly in *Miss Dolly Dollars,* created by Victor Herbert in 1906 to capitalize on Glaser's earlier success with a doll-like character, she never found a suitable replacement for *Varden.* Her much-touted reform of comic opera faded with the dearth of good scripts, and Glaser quickly found herself reverting to her old soubrette ways. The strength of her persona, however, continued to draw substantial audiences despite meager scripts and scores and a decided change in character. The daintiness and delicacy of Dolly was replaced by a boldness and mannishness that some critics found distasteful. This was particularly true in her last great success, *Mlle. Mischief,* which celebrated Glaser's "funny walk" and the deep-throated gurgle that many considered her best asset. Although audiences flocked to see this Shubert-produced vehicle, which was a hit of the 1908–9 season, the press was decidedly reserved. One Chicago critic found her "somewhat too fresh in her gayety" and lectured her against relinquishing feminine instincts in favor of a "too-masculine" temperament. "Miss Glaser flaunts her mannishness and her trousers too proudly," he sniffed, attributing the opera's success to her laugh, which "gurgles through *Mlle. Mischief* with commercial, automatic regularity."[20] Despite critical disapproval, the Glaser gurgle sustained her through three more seasons, albeit unsuccessful, of comic opera, as well as an extended vaudeville tour and even a brief foray into film. How the gurgle was made manifest in a silent film is problematic, although Glaser's energy and open-mouthed smile probably sufficed temporarily but not long enough to sustain a career. By the time early cinema arrived, however, she was ready to retire. In those years she changed husbands, surviving a nasty divorce in which she was sued for alienation of affections by her new husband's ex-wife, and suffered a managerial battle with the Shuberts, who subsequently barred her permanently from appearing in their productions. She did enjoy a few seasons touring with her second husband, Tom Richards, in light vaudeville sketches that, like the comic operas before them, soon ran dry with the lack of worthy new material. By February 1917 the pair was relegated to playing the local vaudeville house in their hometown of Mt. Vernon, New York, when, in an argument over billing, they quit for good. According to Glaser's diary entry for February 10, "we packed our trunk and took a taxi home—and thank God for a home to go to. I'm through with this business and disgusted."[21]

True to her promise to "really retire when I retire," Glaser slipped out of public life. After leaving the stage at forty-three, she lived the remaining forty-one years of her life exactly as planned, happily tucked away on a Connecticut farm surrounded by the books, fine art, and autographed letters she had assiduously collected since her days with Francis Wilson. With the exception of two brief radio appearances and a few profiles in local papers, she was never heard from again.

It is remarkable that Glaser managed to subsist with no discernible income between her retirement in 1917 and her death in 1958. Her second husband, Tom Richards, whom she divorced in 1927 on the grounds of "habitual intemperance," may have brought in some additional income, but he seems to have retired to Connecticut with Glaser shortly after an appearance in the *Ziegfeld Follies of 1917*. Glaser never remarried, and there is no indication of outside support from anyone except her brother, to whom she wrote fairly frequently, particularly in her later years, asking for money.[22] According to correspondence and infrequent interviews, she survived by slowly selling off her books, fine art and collectibles, and all real estate save the Connecticut farm. Although detailed financial records are not extant, it is clear that Glaser must have amassed considerable wealth during her relatively brief career.

In a 1915 interview Glaser regaled a reporter with "Six Rules," posted on her library wall, that serve as an apt description of her theatrical career. According to Glaser, a comedian needs to live life seriously in order to be funny and to meet failure with an unswerving belief in ultimate success. The comedian also needs to cultivate the electric intensity of his or her will by exercising perfect confidence in its ability to attract whatever he or she desires; concurrently, the comedian must develop a belief in financial success by working to perfect a business ideal. And, most important, a comedian needs to nurture individuality by recognizing the invincible character of his or her real self and by putting it before the public at every opportunity.[23] Glaser attributes her success to following these rules and to her steady reliance on "the invincible I." "If one does these things," she asserts, "and cultivates absolutely fearlessness and an unmortgaged independence in thought and action, success ought to come to almost any man or woman."[24]

Is this "invincible I" ultimately the real woman Lulu Glaser sought to become? Did the years of doubt, contradictory impulses, and plain hard work finally pay off in early retirement and a retreat into the world of the self? Glaser achieved what few women of that era could even dream of—financial independence, security through personal real estate holdings, and a rarified collection of scholarly and artistic works. Her achievements, although at times aided by various men, certainly were not male reliant. She always had a strained relationship with her father, who died in 1913, and both her marriages failed. Only Wilson's support and influence was long lasting, but even that seemed to disappear after Glaser was about seven years into her solo career. The stage may not have been the place for "real women," but, at least for Glaser, it provided a means to an end and the fulfillment of a truly independent life.

Notes

1. Lulu Glaser, "Home, Not the Stage, and the Place for Real Women," manuscript, c. 1907, Princeton. Subsequent quotations from this source are referenced parenthetically in the text as "Home."

2. Unidentified scrapbook clipping, Lulu Glaser Collection, William Seymour Theatre Collection, Firestone Library, Princeton University. All quotations, unless otherwise cited, are from this collection. I am grateful to Princeton

University Library for permission to quote from various items in this collection, hereafter cited as Princeton.

3. [note to come]

4. Martha Schmoyer LoMonaco, "Lulu Glaser and the Fad for Comic Opera," *Princeton University Library Chronicle* 48, no. 1 (autumn 1986): 66–67, 68, 70. The *Princeton University Library Chronicle* has kindly granted permission to quote the previous two paragraphs from my article.

5. "Judge's Favorites," unidentified scrapbook clipping, Princeton.

6. Unidentified clipping, *Mlle. Mischief* file, Princeton.

7. Percy Hammond, *Chicago Post,* n.d., Princeton.

8. Clipping, *Chicago Record Herald,* n.d., Princeton.

9. Clipping, *Chicago Journal,* n.d., Princeton.

10. Unidentified clippings, *Detroit Journal* and *Boston Traveler,* n.d., Princeton.

11. Francis Wilson to Lulu Glaser, May 27, 1896, Princeton.

12. Unidentified clipping, "Lulu Glaser, a Woman of Contrasts," June 22, 1901, Scrapbook 246, Lulu Glaser, vol. 1, Robinson Locke Collection, Billy Rose Theatre Collection, New York Public Library for the Performing Arts.

13. Unidentified clippings, January 19, 1902, Scrapbook 246, Lulu Glaser, vol. 1, Robinson Locke Collection, Billy Rose Theatre Collection, New York Public Library for the Performing Arts.

14. Lulu Glaser to Fred C. Whitney, December 5, 1902, Princeton.

15. Charles Dillingham to Lulu Glaser, January 25, 1906, Princeton.

16. Unidentified clipping, *Dolly Varden* file, Princeton.

17. Unidentified clipping, "Timely Chats with Stars," Lulu Glaser collection, Princeton.

18. Unidentified clipping, *Dolly Varden* file, Princeton.

19. Ibid.

20. Clipping, *Chicago Inter Ocean,* n.d., Princeton.

21. Lulu Glaser, Diary 1917–19, Princeton.

22. Glaser correspondence files, 1925–58, Princeton.

23. Peter Pepper, "A Drink of Iced Tea with Lulu Glaser," *Moving Picture Weekly,* August 7, 1915, Princeton.

24. Ibid.

Women and the Benefit

"Peculiar Constructions" and Representations of Gendered Communities

Helen Huff

T HE AMERICAN THEATRE of the nineteenth century was one of the few occupations that offered white women an equitable salary and a relatively safe working environment.[1] Yet even here women encountered the dominant gender ideology that created a theatrical fare constructed around male subjects in male-centered dramas. However, the theatre also had a performance site where women could "act" together and construct temporary sites of collective activity. In the theatrical benefit women formed voluntary associations that opened avenues to empowerment and agency.

Although several characteristics mark the benefit performance as decidedly different from regular performances, this essay will focus on the role of gender in the benefit.[2] A gender analysis of the benefit reveals that it operated as a communal organization that, although temporary, offered space for a new representation of gender and created more opportunities for women. Benefits combined traditional social elements associated with women, such as communal reciprocity and voluntarism, with direct economic agency and power and allowed women to bypass the patriarchal system of representation dominant in the nineteenth-century theatre. They operated as female-centered, entrepreneurial performance sites that highlighted female subjectivity, featured more roles for women than did the traditional repertoire, and allowed women to support their own causes and concerns. Ultimately, the benefit offered a site where localized communities of women could temporarily transgress and resist the patriarchal canon and create new gendered representations.[3]

Briefly, the benefit system consisted of two basic types, the contractual benefit and the charity benefit. The contractual benefit performance was a form of compensation for actors in the theatre in which proceeds of the evening were given to the particular performer. Relatively free from managerial control, the actor chose the play, or plays, and scenes or roles played and cast the plays as she desired. Charity benefits were performed to give financial aid to others: actors in the community who were ill or destitute, families of deceased actors, and concerns and causes in the greater society.

Two specific elements marked all benefits: reciprocity and voluntarism. Reciprocal exchange—the giving of a favor with the promise of future repayment—often referred to as mutual aid or cooperation, was crucial to the enormous success of the benefit system because actors were not paid to appear in each other's benefits. Actors practiced reciprocity as a form of social and professional "currency," which they used to negotiate with each other and to support each other and the benefit system. Anthropologists argue that this form of "benevolent help" is crucial to small communities that are denied power in the larger community because more aid provided to community members helps the entire community. In fact, many women's historians have argued that during the nineteenth century, small, local community institutions such as women's benevolent associations used these very principles of reciprocity, trust, and cooperation to achieve a sense of power and autonomy within the larger society.[4]

The nineteenth-century theatre was also a site where reciprocity was crucial to a community. Many actors spoke of the benefit as a place where "the most generous spirit of appreciation and mutual assistance among actors" existed. Performers knew the importance of mutual aid and reciprocity in maintaining the empowering benefit system, often mentioning the "fixed rule amongst performers, to lend each other every help they can in time of benefits." Actress Clara Morris speaks of the "warmness and easy familiarity, a trust and mutual aid" actors extended to each other. This mutual aid is dependent on some degree of equal power. In the benefit, marked by the absence of the theatrical manager and his "rules," there was a greater degree of shared power between performers than in the regular season. Even stars understood the power of reciprocity, and most were careful to maintain reciprocal ties to supporting actors.[5]

Voluntarism was crucial to both the benefit system and nineteenth-century women's culture. It helped to maintain stability and cohesion as a form of "social glue" that held communities together, nurturing a sense of communal spirit and well-being. Voluntarism enabled the benefit system to survive for hundreds of years, with men and women supporting each other as volunteers, and benefit playbills reflect this crucial role by foregrounding the rhetoric of "thanking" and announcing volunteers. They often marked the word *volunteer* in large, boldface type or in all capital letters, and beneficiaries often featured their volunteers in starring roles.[6]

Although reciprocity and voluntarism applied to benefits of both male and female actors, gender-specific voluntarism and reciprocity appears to be a much more frequent phenomenon in women's benefits. More significantly, men's benefits used the same plays as in the traditional repertoire, with female volunteers simply repeating the supporting parts they regularly played. Thus, men's benefits typically re-inscribed the same gendered subject system. Women's benefits, however, followed a distinctly different pattern, one that foregrounded a greater variety of women's roles.

For example, benefits frequently featured a "principal volunteer," an actor or actress who played a major leading role in a scene or scenes. In the benefits of women this principal volunteer was often another woman. Because the traditional canon featured more male/female two-person scenes than female/female, this presented a unique circumstance for the two actresses. Women used different strategies to deal with this situation. One such strategy was for one actress to play the male role. At the Bowery Theatre, during the 1849–50 season, both Caroline Wemyss and Mrs. J. W. Wallack Jr. (Ann Sefton) appeared together during the season. Wallack excelled in playing older leading roles and Wemyss, new to the theatre, played younger supporting roles in dramas. During the Bowery season they appeared as "principal volunteers" in each other's benefits. At each benefit they staged *Romeo and Juliet* with Wemyss portraying Juliet and Wallack taking on the role of Romeo, a role she frequently played in benefits. Wemyss and Wallack had a history of supporting each other in benefits. During the 1847 Bowery season, Wemyss had made her "first appearance in comedy" during a benefit for Wallack (then known as Mrs. John Sefton). The presence of female "principal volunteers" may help explain the prevalence of such inversion (females playing male roles), a hallmark of the benefit.[7]

Moreover, because actors were free to select what plays or scenes they wished for their benefit and to cast as they pleased, women could create a performance that reflected their concerns and interests. For the freewheeling "one night only" of the benefit, a performance by women could feature a degree of subject positioning unknown in the regular repertoire. These performances might feature a new play written by a woman, often specifically for that benefit. One of America's earliest female playwrights, Susannah Rowson, wrote what is arguably her most famous play, *Slaves in Algiers,* for her family's annual benefit performance while she was in the New American Company of Wignell and Reinagle. Not only does this play feature five substantial female roles, but the role of Rebecca is a strong female presence easily on a par with the male roles. Moreover, the epilogue of the play, spoken by Rowson (who appears to have played Rebecca in the original benefit), is directed to the women in the audience. This direct appeal to female spectators— another hallmark of women's benefits—could serve to enlarge the community of women in the theatre the night of the benefit. Rowson's other plays—*The Female Patriot, The American Tar,* and *Americans in England*—were also written for family benefits and highlighted strong women in the leading roles, usually played by Rowson.[8]

Producing their own plays in their own benefits, actresses assumed the producer's risk for the new play. After the success of *Slaves in Algiers* in the original benefit production, producers Wignell and Reinagle entered the play into the company's repertoire. In this way the actress could persuade an otherwise reluctant theatre manager to produce her play, a play often featuring more female roles than normally found in the repertoire. For her benefits actress/playwright Charlotte Barnes created several new plays featuring strong female roles, including many breeches roles for her. Her most famous play, *Octavia Bragaldi,* was originally written for her father's benefit with Charlotte in the title role. It went on to successful runs in almost every major city in the United States and was repeated in London and Liverpool. The central subject of the play is the loving relationship between Octavia and her second husband. The strong focus on this domestic relationship creates a more female-centered play.[9]

Female stars frequently commissioned plays to be written expressly for their benefits. Julia Daly, a popular star of the 1860s, obviously wanted to partake in the lucrative commodity of *Our American Cousin* when she commissioned a play entitled *Our American Female Cousin* for her 1862 Winter Garden benefit. Instead of the traditional male hero of Taylor's play, Daly's play featured a female character in the role of the protagonist. There is no evidence to show that this play ever entered a regular repertoire, or indeed, was ever performed outside of Daly's benefit. It does demonstrate, however, the power of the benefit as a site where women could rewrite anything for their own pleasure and agency. Classical plays were included in that agency. Mary Gannon, a popular "light" comedy star at the Bowery and the Olympic, attempted Congreve's *Love for Love* in an 1860 benefit, advertising the fact that she was "carefully revising, curtailing, and altering" the play. The possibilities of authorial adaptation in the benefit were so powerful that stars could even change their most popular vehicles. Clara Morris, including her popular *Camille* in a benefit, cut several pages from the death scene in the last act, thinking the audience was "too excited to contain itself." She explained that "never would I have dared to do such a thing had it been for more than one performance." To do this outside of the benefit performance would have put the action under the dominance of the manager and would have constituted a clear violation of management rules.[10]

Women frequently included plays in their benefits that were never seen in the regular, male-dominated repertoire. Many of these pieces featured not only more roles for women but sometimes only female roles. Perhaps because of this very female-centered subjectivity these plays were marked by rhetoric denoting "first time this season" or "never acted here." For example, Mrs. Brougham, wife of prolific actor/ playwright John Brougham, included *The Ladies' Club,* an anonymous, all-female comedy, in her 1853 benefit at Wallack's Lyceum. The play recreated a ladies' club meeting, featured six substantial roles for women, and had the largest number of women's roles of any piece during the season. It was so popular with audiences that it was repeated in Mrs. Brougham's second benefit a month later, an unusual occurrence. Not surprisingly, however, in a company that featured three male actors to every one female actor, the play did not appear in the regular Wallack repertoire. At the same theatre Mrs. Vernon, appearing there in 1866, included in her benefit "for the first time, a comedy of peculiar construction, the cast consisting ENTIRELY OF LADIES, entitled *Ladies at Home,*" which utilized all the women in the company and did not appear during the rest of the season.[11]

Benefits frequently featured decontextualized scenes. Women's use of these isolated scenes marked a crucial difference in constructing a female-centered performance because men very seldom used this strategy. It could be argued that men simply did not need to construct their benefit evenings in this manner because the traditional canon already featured plays that were male centered. Nevertheless, a female beneficiary could "cut and paste" an evening of selected two-person scenes from traditional plays in the repertoire that featured a female character, usually in the "act of highest passion" or some equally climactic moment for the character. For example, the "sleepwalking" scene from *Macbeth*, featuring Lady Macbeth; the "trial" scene from *The Merchant of Venice*, featuring Portia; and the "recognition" scene from *The Stranger*, highlighting Mrs. Haller, were all frequently used by women in their benefits. By taking these selected scenes, which highlighted a female character, out of the context of the original play, the female character became the subject of the scene. In this sense the beneficiary performer became the playwright, or author, as she produced and staged these new performance texts that collapsed distinguishing dramaturgical structures to blur the traditional boundaries of playwright and performer. These new performance texts could shift focus, at least temporarily, to a new female-centered paradigm of performance, one that displaced the male subject and substituted a female one, foregrounding gender, and changing the inscribed position of woman from object to subject. One example of an anonymous playbill gives a distilled illustration of that model. It highlights four two-person scenes from Shakespeare—Ophelia and Hamlet, Anne and Richard II, Desdemona and Othello, and Juliet and Romeo—and features the same female performer playing all the female roles and different male actors in each scene. By using this strategy, women disrupted and displaced the structure of traditional play texts and restructured them into new performance texts that upset traditional subject positions.[12]

Female audiences turned out for these female-centered events. Direct appeals to women were sometimes located in the plays themselves, such as Rowson's appeal to women in the epilogue of *Slaves in Algiers*. Newspaper accounts, however, also provide evidence of the gendered community possible in women's benefits. At a benefit for Mrs. Coleman Pope at the Academy of Music in 1857 the featured play of the evening was *Romeo and Juliet*, with Coleman Pope playing Romeo and her principal volunteer, Mrs. McMahon, playing Juliet. Newspaper critics said "the house was comfortably filled, with a very orderly, intelligent, and even fashionable audience, including many ladies, a majority of whom were doubtless drawn together by a feeling of curiosity, and the rest might safely be set down as the personal friends and admirers of the heroine of the evening." In an after-curtain thank-you speech to the audience Coleman Pope specifically thanked the women in the audience for attending and supporting her. Yet another newspaper review reported that actress/manager Laura Keene "thanked the ladies for their powerful support" after an 1856 benefit at her theatre. Last, in a newspaper review on a benefit for dancer Fanny Essler the author noted that the benches of the pit had been converted into stalls to accommodate the increased female presence in the audience, "just for this night," a condition that Essler noted was "an unusual sight, for only men were usually admitted there."[13]

When an entire season of benefits at one theatre is examined, it becomes apparent that the female benefit regularly offered more performance opportunities for women. For example, the 1839–40 season at Mitchell's Olympic Theatre featured twenty-one benefits, five of which were for women. These five benefits included proportionately more women's roles than any regular-season performances. A similar pattern existed at Wallack's. The women of the company selected plays that not only featured female subjects but also included more roles for women than found in the regular repertoire. For example, they frequently selected plays written by women that highlighted female subjects, such as Hannah Cowley's *A Bold Stroke for a Husband,* a play with five substantial female roles, a rarity at Wallack's and not seen in the regular season. Cowley's *The Belle's Stratagem* was also popular in women's benefits, featuring six substantial female roles. Three plays—*The Youthful Queen; Mary, Queen of Scots;* and *Two Queens*—were frequently performed in women's benefits, featured strong female subjects (Mary, Queen of Scots; Queen Christina of Sweden; and Mary, Queen of Denmark), and were not found in the regular repertoire. Again, perhaps this very emphasis on female subjectivity, along with the plays' lack of male roles, made them unpopular with managers and male actors. Nevertheless, given that female actors, like their male counterparts, desired to make as much money as they could in their benefits, the continued use of these plays must have reflected their popularity with audiences, or the actresses would have discontinued them.[14]

Patterns of female benefit communities are also found in the working-class theatres—the Chatham and the Bowery. Fanny Herring, a principal at both theatres during the 1850s and 1860s, employed similar strategies. Her benefits featured more female volunteers and more roles for women. Her popular cross-dressed piece, *Jack Sheppard,* was frequently performed at female Bowery benefits, often with markedly different casting than the regular-season performances. An 1856 benefit featured three different actresses playing Jack in each of the play's three acts. In addition, the Bowery female benefit community extended to the ballet corps, extensive at this theatre. Ballet "girls" were paid low wages and seldom, if ever, had a benefit. The principal women of the Bowery frequently included musical numbers highlighting this group in their benefits. In fact, playbills of several women's benefits listed the corps as "principal volunteers" for the evening. Men's benefits from these theatres do not include any selected pieces that offer agency to this female group.[15]

Gendered communities also used the charity benefit to support causes or concerns. In the theatre community male performers tended to be more involved in communal aid for traditional male causes, whereas female performers supported women's causes more strongly. For example, men supported traditionally masculine groups such as the Elks and the Masons—both mutual-aid societies that were closed to women— whereas women supported more female-identified organizations such as moral reform and benevolent organizations for women and children. Both men and women extended gender-specific support to each other.[16] The remainder of this essay will briefly discuss the female-oriented charity benefit matinee and three different charity benefit strategies used by women in the theatre.

Female managers Laura Keene in Manhattan and Sarah Crocker Conway in Brooklyn created and popularized the charity benefit matinee. They shrewdly picked up on the attendance of women at midday performances and capitalized on women's connection to charity by using these events to raise money for certain causes. Keene organized well-attended benefit matinees for women, and Conway presented "Ladies Matinees" for charity, such as an 1874 benefit matinee "in aid of the poor of Brooklyn." In an advertisement typical of charity benefits by women, Conway's playbills noted in large, bold typeface "the entire proceeds devoted to the above charity!" Keene and her charity benefit matinees clearly targeted fashionable, white, society women who found a welcome atmosphere as they "flocked to her theatre to raise funds for their various functions." Moreover, Keene was careful to create a private space for female matinee attendees in her theatre, including separate lounges for men and women. Conway, who managed and acted at Brooklyn's Park Theatre (1864–71) and her own Brooklyn Theatre (1871–75), also specifically targeted women in advertisements for matinee performances. One such handbill pitched an Election Day matinee: "Ladies you can vote. Buy your tickets at the box office, Park Theatre, for election afternoon matinee. Repeaters invited to vote often. Your vote taken. No registry required. Vote often, is our mottos [sic]. Tickets only 15, 25 and 50 cents, which gives you a vote, and also a brilliant entertainment at the Park Theatre election day matinee. A Grand Double Bill."[17]

The benefit was also used as a charity fund-raising tool for nationwide causes and organizations in which women were interested. One such group was the Mount Vernon Association (MVA). The MVA was a voluntary group of women who had banded together to prevent the sale of Mount Vernon, the family home of George Washington, which was in disrepair and on the auction block. In 1854, after her retirement from the stage, actress/playwright Anna Cora Mowatt was approached to join the organization and to spearhead its campaign to purchase the Washington estate. Mowatt, elected secretary of the central committee, used her position in the theatrical community to raise money for the association by organizing several early fund-raising benefits for the cause. She also enlisted the aid of other theatrical women to coordinate a major fund-raising drive that lasted over nine years, until the purchase and renovation was completed in 1864. Laura Keene organized one of the largest benefits for this association in late 1858 and aimed this matinee benefit at women and children by appealing directly to them in the playbill. The "ladies of the MVA committee" responded favorably to this benefit, and *Godey's Lady's Book,* the social arbiter of middle- and upper-class women, gave its approval to the effort by printing the names of givers in its monthly magazine, emphasizing that "ladies" were raising the funds. Women of the theatrical community offered another benefit for the MVA in December 1863. Held at the large, ornate Academy of Music, this "Grand Gala Festival" lasted three days. Tickets were $1 for the entire three-day affair, but 25¢ tickets were available "in order that all classes of the community may have an opportunity of contributing their mite [*sic*] to this national homage." The bill of fare featured a wide cross-section of theatrical entertainment, ranging from Matilda Heron, appearing in *Medea,* to minstrel sketches, opera arias, and songs and musical "melanges."[18]

Theatrical women also used the charity benefit for more personal means: to raise money for fellow female performers who were ill or destitute. Two of these large-scale benefits deserve mention. A female-sponsored "complimentary" benefit held for Clara Fisher Maeder in 1841 raised over $2,000. Fisher Maeder, born in England in 1811, had been a popular child star who had made a fortune in the theatre and had retired when she married. After the marriage Fisher Maeder's fortune transferred to her husband. In the financial panic of 1841 Maeder's husband lost the money, and the former child star found herself struggling to reestablish a performing career as an adult. Wishing to help, a "committee of ladies," all of whom were actresses, organized a benefit at the Park Theatre on September 28, 1841. To avoid the stigma of charitable aid, the women called it a "complimentary" benefit and advertised it as "originating in the minds, and successfully carried on to performance by the exertions solely of the ladies, and moreover, the very first complimentary benefit that ever was given to a lady in this country." The playbills for this event clearly mark it as a voluntary effort put forth by women.[19]

One of Laura Keene's last projects in the theatre community was to produce and direct a massive "monster" benefit for actress Matilda Heron. "Monster," or collective, benefits were highly communal in nature and frequently featured several theatres joining together for performances, the proceeds of which would go to the individual or charity organization. Heron, one of the biggest stars of the midcentury because of her acclaimed performance as Camille, had become ill and was penniless, and the theatrical community rallied to her aid. Specifically, women of the community, many of whom had worked with Heron since the 1850s, sponsored the benefit in January 1872 at the Academy of Music. Performers from theatres all over the city participated, and Keene herself, although very ill, presented the first act of *The School for Scandal*. In her correspondence Keene referred to it as an "ultra fashionable charity matinee." It was a standing-room-only event and brought in almost $5,400, a huge sum at the time.[20]

Whether performed under contract or for charity, benefits offered theatrical women a place to form temporary communities that used traditionally female strategies of voluntarism and gender-specific reciprocity to bypass the patriarchal system of representation. In the benefit women were able to break through barriers of containment constructed by the dominant gender ideology and create "peculiar constructions" that allowed a different representation of gender on the nineteenth-century stage. These representations allowed a variety of spectators to "see" new constructs throughout the century and allowed theatrical women to create female-dominated performance sites. Moreover, the benefit served to bind the theatrical women's community together in the nineteenth century and to extend mutual aid and support to each other in times of crisis.

Notes

1. For information on salaries and working conditions see Bessie Rayner Parkes, *Essays on Women's Work* (London: A. Strahan, 1865): Edna Hammer Cooley, "Women in American Theatre, 1850–1870: A Study in Professional Equity" (Ph.D. diss., University of Maryland–College Park, 1986); David L. Rinear, *The Temple of Momus: Mitchell's Olympic Theatre* (Metuchen, N.J.:

Scarecrow Press, 1987), 41–47; Olive Logan, *Before the Footlights and Behind the Scenes* (Philadelphia: Parmelee, 1870), 93.

2. Characteristics of benefits include a reliance on voluntarism and reciprocity among players, the performers as producer and/or author, the possibility of inversion as a transgressive instrument, a highly complex interplay of theatrical elements, and an emphasis on the cultivation of audience appeal and patronage. These elements, although used by all actors, were manipulated very differently by women and men.

3. It is beyond the scope of this essay to address the myriad elements of the benefit system and how they operated to reflect social constructs. My purpose here is simply to argue the possibility of an alternative gender ideology located in the benefit.

4. See Matthew Ridley, *The Origins of Virtue: Human Instincts and the Evolution of Cooperation* (New York: Viking, 1996), 200–262, for an excellent discussion of how reciprocal altruism operates in human societies. See also Lawrence C. Becker, *Reciprocity* (Chicago: University of Chicago Press, 1986); and Armen Albert Alchian, ed., *The Economics of Charity* (London: Institute of Economic Affairs, 1973). To situate this argument in women's history, see Christine Bolt, *The Women's Movements in the United States and Britain from the 1790s to the 1920s* (Amherst: University of Massachusetts Press, 1993); Lori D. Ginzberg, *Women and the Work of Benevolence: Morality, Politics, and Class in the Nineteenth-Century United States* (New Haven, Conn.: Yale University Press, 1990); Glenna Matthews, *Woman's Power and Woman's Place in the United States, 1630–1970* (New York: Oxford, 1992).

5. See Frederick Warde, *Fifty Years of Make-Believe* (New York: International Press Syndicate, 1920), 42–43; Clara Morris, *Life on the Stage: My Personal Experiences and Recollections* (New York: McCLure, Phillips, 1891), 180.

6. For information on voluntary women's associations see Mary Ann Clawson, "Nineteenth-Century Women's Auxiliaries and Fraternal Orders," *Signs: Journal of Women in Culture and Society* 12 (autumn 1986): 1; Kathleen D. McCarthy, *Noblesse Oblige: Charity and Cultural Philanthropy in Chicago, 1849–1929* (Chicago: University of Chicago Press, 1982); and Rosemarie Bank, *Theatre Culture in America, 1825–1860* (New York: Cambridge University Press, 1997), 101–51. For information on moral reform societies and temperance and abolition activities by women see Beverly Gordon, *Bazaars and Fair Ladies: The History of the American Fundraising Fair* (Knoxville: University of Tennessee Press, 1998); Nancy F. Cott, *The Bonds of Womanhood: "Woman's Sphere" in New England, 1780–1835* (New Haven, Conn.: Yale University Press, 1977).

7. Playbills, Bowery Theatre, Oct. 24, 1849, and March 29, 1850, Harvard Theatre Collection (hereafter cited as HTC); Playbill, Bowery Theatre, June 12, 1847, Billy Rose Theatre Collection, New York Public Library. Although such inversion was sometimes found in the regular repertoire, it was a much more frequent phenomenon in women's benefits.

8. Amelia Howe Kritzer, *Plays by American Women, 1775–1850* (Ann Arbor: University of Michigan Press, 1995), 7–12, 55–95.

9. Ibid., 24.

10. Playbill, Winter Garden Theatre, July 18, 1862, HTC; Playbill, Wallack's Theatre, April 11, 1869, Lincoln Center Library for the Performing Arts, New York Public Library; Morris, *Life on the Stage*, 386.

11. Playbills, Wallack's Lyceum Theatre, March 19, April 29, 1853, HTC.

12. Undated benefit playbill, Drury Lane, benefits clipping file, Lincoln Center Library for the Performing Arts, New York Public Library.

13. Playbill, Academy of Music, Jan. 17, 1857, and undated *Spirit of the Times* review, both found in the scrapbook of Mrs. Frank Rea, New York Public Library; Playbill, Laura Keene's Theatre, June 21, 1856, HTC; *New York Times* review, June 23, 1856; Ivor Guest, *Fanny Essler* (Middletown, Conn.: Wesleyan University Press, 1970), 115.

14. Playbills, Mitchell's Olympic Theatre, Dec. 1839–40, HTC; Playbills, Wallack's Theatre, 1854–1864, Lincoln Center Library for the Performing Arts, New York Public Library. Because actors frequently did not list authors of plays on benefit playbills, the authorship of these three plays is not verifiable. Charles Shannon is the only author listed in bibliographic sources for a play titled *The Youthful Queen* (1828). John Baldwin Buckstone is likely the author of *Two Queens* (1837), and several authors are listed for plays with the title *Mary, Queen of Scots*. The most frequently mentioned play of this title I was able to find in bibliographic sources is by W. H. W. Murray, but none of these sources gives a date of publication.

15. Playbill, Bowery Theatre, Aug. 15, 1856, HTC. *Jack Sheppard* was originally written as a cross-dressed role for Mary Ann Keeley, an English actress, but was quickly appropriated by men. Nevertheless, it was frequently performed cross-dressed in women's benefits. Playbills, Bowery Theatre, Jan. 16, 1857, and Chatham Theatre, Feb. 6, 1857, HTC.

16. This is yet another element of benefit analysis that is beyond the scope of this essay. Although charity benefits strongly follow gender-specific constructions, contractual benefits were more complex. The construction of popular appeal sometimes required women to form communal bonds with groups that included men, such as volunteer fire companies. Many actresses used the benefit to nurture these ties and relationships. Another intriguing question for analysis is how did spectators—both male and female—view these performances of gender? How did gender and sexuality affect their reception? Did men and women view them the same way?

17. Playbill, Mrs. Conway's Brooklyn Theatre, April 7, 1874, HTC; Vernanne Bryan, *Laura Keene: A British Actress on the American Stage, 1826–1873* (Jefferson, N.C.: McFarland, 1997), 84; Handbill, Conway's Park Theatre, Nov. 7, year unknown, HTC.

18. The women of the MVA were turned down when they approached the owners to buy the property because women could not legally own property at

the time. It was suggested that they seek incorporation and have the corporation complete the sale. To become incorporated, however, any organization in Virginia had to have its charter approved by the state. Although no laws specifically barred women's organizations from incorporating, no charter approval had ever been issued to these groups, and no women's organizations had ever been incorporated. Mowatt, working with the Central Committee, drew up a charter and began campaigning in early 1855 to get it passed by the Virginia legislature. The women faced the obstacle of antifemale prejudice in the state House but persevered, and the charter bill was finally passed on March 19, 1856. For the first time in the United States women had a lawful basis to band together for legal, contractual action. The Mount Vernon estate, bought by the now-titled Mount Vernon Ladies' Association for the Union, would be maintained as a "philanthropic, educational and patriotic enterprise." See Eric Wollencott Barnes, *The Lady of Fashion: The Life and the Theatre of Anna Cora Mowatt* (New York: Scribner's Sons, 1954), 266–82; Playbill, HTC, Laura Keene's Theatre, Dec. 28, 1858; Keene to managers of the MVLA, Dec. 14, 1858, HTC, Laura Keene file; Playbill, Academy of Music, Dec. 1863, HTC.

19. *New York Herald,* Sep. 29, 1841; Playbill, Park Theatre, Sep. 28, 1841, HTC.

20. Playbill, Academy of Music, Jan. 17, 1872, HTC; Bryan, *Laura Keene,* 162.

Breeches and Blondes

Nineteenth-Century Theatrical
and Cultural Performance

Kirsten Pullen

> There is no trick in Miss Cushman's performance; no thought, no interest, no feeling, seems to actuate her, except what might be looked for in Romeo himself were Romeo reality.
>
> —*Spirit of the Times*

> Female face and form carry all [*The Forty Thieves'*] honors, and in idiotic parody of masculinity create its uproarious mirth.
>
> —*New York Times*

THESE TWO REVIEWS, one of thespian Charlotte Cushman, the other of burlesquer Lydia Thompson, demonstrate how audiences and critics variously read the cross-dressed nineteenth-century actress. Cushman and Thompson's careers were separated by about a generation, played to different audiences, and specialized in different kinds of breeches acting. In this essay I want to examine correspondences between their careers to highlight the specific problems Victorian actresses faced, especially those whose careers and lifestyles seemed to challenge Victorian American ideologies of gender. Cushman convincingly portrayed male characters; her Hamlet, Romeo, and Cardinal Wolsey were critically designated as completely "male" performances. Lydia Thompson, on the other hand, used male clothing and attitudes to highlight her femininity. Audiences did not believe her impersonation of masculinity; rather, many critics were alarmed precisely by Thompson's blurred distinctions between male and female. Cross-dressed— albeit in tights, short pants, and tight corsets—Thompson talked like a man but walked like a woman. She was neither fully male nor female but, in the words of critic William Dean Howells "an alien sex, parodying both."[1] In short, Cushman's performances basically adhered to a binary understanding of gender, whereas Thompson's threatened the stability of that binary.

This understanding of gender corresponds to the Victorian Cult of True Womanhood, the notion that a "true woman" was pious, sensitive, emotional, and dependent. Her "natural" role was as wife and mother, and her natural sphere was the family and home.[2] This trope of the middle class attempted to relegate women to a passive position, as help-mates to their husbands, suggesting that women who wanted societal approval and the financial security provided by marriage subsume their own desires within their husband's more public agendas.[3] It is impor-tant to note, however, the contradictions inherent in the Cult of True Womanhood; this discourse was neither seamless nor absolute.[4] In short, it influenced women's lives but did not determine them.

Contrasting Cushman's and Thompson's different roles and pub-lic personas highlights the constitutive place female sexuality held in American theatre during the Victorian era. In particular, the breeches role reveals how the representation of femininity and female sexuality registers in nineteenth-century theatre. Although Lawrence Levine, for example, uses (male) class conflict to distinguish between "high" and "low" theatrical entertainments, I argue here that the display of fe-male sexuality also participated in this hierarchization.[5] Attention to female performers demonstrates how the Cult of True Womanhood in-fluenced theatre reception; the representation of femininity and fe-male sexuality distinguished between legitimate and illegitimate per-formances.

That such distinctions existed at all testifies to the upward mobility of the theatre profession.[6] By the middle of the nineteenth century, actors and actresses in the United States and Great Britain were usually treated as skillful, legitimate artists. However, Victorian actresses con-tinued to be limited by gendered expectations about the kinds of roles they could play, the kinds of private and public lives they should lead, and the kinds of sexuality they might embody onstage.[7] Further, the increased professionalization of the legitimate theatre was achieved in part by strictly dividing performers into two camps: those who per-fected their art through years of training and apprenticeship and per-formed both classics of the theatrical canon and contemporary master-pieces against those who, with little formal training, sang, danced, and told jokes. Where once all theatre was viewed as suspect and profane, by the nineteenth century a hierarchy was established that distinguished between morally uplifting, educational entertainments and morally bankrupt, spectacular productions. For actresses in particular, this distinction had little to do with popularity—both legitimate actresses such as Fanny Kemble and spectacular performers such as Adah Isaacs Menken commanded high salaries and performed for large audiences—and much to do with notions of taste, refinement, and artistic value informed by notions of appropriate female sexual behavior and representation. As the experiences of Cushman and Thompson demonstrate, a realistic presentation of masculinity marked the performance as legitimate.

Cushman and Thompson present interesting case studies in the relationship between breeches roles and ideologies of gender on the nineteenth-century stage. Although Cushman's and Thompson's careers followed very different trajectories, they shared salient correspondences I want to pursue here. Both were powerful women who managed their own careers and used the press and other publicity apparatuses to frame their public personas. Both struggled against the ideological precepts of the Cult of True Womanhood while fashioning their careers and public selves, albeit in different ways. A look at their respective biographies indicates a crucial distinction: Cushman framed her acting career within domestic ideology and so was rewarded on the legitimate stage, whereas Thompson challenged that ideology through her performances and publicity.

Charlotte Cushman (1818–76) was the first American actress to achieve critical and financial success equal to European stars; in addition to creating memorable female characters, she played more than forty male roles during her long career.[8] As a teenager she performed as a vocal soloist and opera singer but turned to the stage in 1836 after losing her singing voice. She debuted as Lady Macbeth in New Orleans, returned to Boston and New York, and built a career in the United States playing strong, tortured women such as Nancy Sykes, Lady Macbeth, and Meg Merrilies, as well as male Shakespearean heroes such as Hamlet and Romeo. In 1844 she played Lady Macbeth opposite British giant William Charles Macready; after this success she spent a triumphant two seasons in London, reprising that role and adding Queen Katharine from Shakespeare's *Henry VIII*, Bianca in *Fazio*, Meg Merrilies, Romeo, and Hamlet. She continued to tour England, the United States, and Europe, retiring more than once after a profitable farewell tour until her death on February 18, 1876. From the 1840s until her death she was critically and financially successful, ultimately commanding salaries on par with her male costars Macready, Edwin Forrest, and Edwin Booth. Hundreds attended her funeral. Politicians, writers, critics, performers, and average men and women mobbed her funeral procession in an out-pouring of grief and recognition.[9]

Lydia Thompson (1836–1908), as star and comanager of the burlesque troupe the British Blondes,[10] introduced all-female burlesque to the United States. The Blondes debuted at George Wood's Metropolitan Theatre and Museum in August 1868. The details of Thompson's life before her American tour are sparsely documented: dates, productions, and liaisons are variously attributed or omitted, especially regarding her age and marital status. Thompson first appeared as the title heroine in the 1846 Christmas pageant *Little Silver Hair* when she was ten years old.[11] In 1854 she challenged a Spanish dancer (La Perea, or Perea Nina) to a competition, matching her step for step and endearing herself to patriotic British audiences. Thompson toured Great Britain and much of continental Europe from 1855 to 1865, gradually moving from "straight" plays to more daring song-and-dance routines. She married Alexander Henderson in 1868, and he began managing Thompson and her blonde costars Pauline Markham, Alice Logan, Ada Harland, Lisa Walker, and lone male troupe member Harry Beckett. They premiered the burlesques *Ixion, or the Man at the Wheel, Ernani,* and *The Forty Thieves* in New York in 1868–69. In the 1870s the Blondes toured throughout the United States, with Thompson frequently playing the leading male role. In their first season the British Blondes were an unparalleled theatrical success; their New York season and subsequent tour sold out most shows, and several imitation burlesque troupes sprang up, mimicking the Blondes' physical and theatrical style. This approval was short-lived, however; within six months of their debut the Blondes, and burlesque in general, were subjected to heavy criticism from both theatrical critics and social commentators: burlesque had become a "plague," threatening to contaminate middle-class theatregoers with immorality and bad taste.[12] Despite this disapproval Thompson and the Blondes continued to perform; Thompson toured regularly until the late 1880s and performed sporadically until her death on November 17, 1908, in London.

Both women enjoyed their tremendous success in part because of their relentless self-promotion. Cushman and Thompson used the press to disseminate positive information about their families, fan base, and romantic status. This construction of personas is crucial to understanding why audiences and critics responded differently to their theatrical cross-dressing and clarifies distinctions between legitimate and illegitimate theatre circuits. Because a full discussion of their careers is beyond the scope of this essay, I will focus on four specific points of analysis—

their reasons for beginning a theatrical career, their marital status, their cross-dressed roles, and their publicity photos—to contrast how each framed herself as a woman and a performer in relation to the nineteenth-century notion of "True Womanhood."

Charlotte Cushman described her early theatrical career as a sacrifice made to save her family from poverty and destitution. When she was fifteen, her father died, leaving the family in debt. Charlotte, who characterized herself as a tomboy, began singing in Ralph Waldo Emerson's Boston Unitarian Church in order to prepare for a professional career while receiving a small salary.[13] Cushman made much of her beginnings as a singer rather than as an actress. Throughout her life she claimed that only the loss of her voice forced her onto the stage; if she had been able to continue in opera, she would never have needed to play such dramatic, masculine roles. In addition, her stories of her early life and family background stressed her family's gentility. Cushman frequently mentioned that her father was descended from Mayflower passengers, focused on her middle-class upbringing and education, and suggested her Christian values had been forged as a member of Emerson's famous church.[14] In this way Cushman maintained an air of respectability despite her choice of a theatrical career. She always explained that circumstance rather than desire had forced her to make her way onto the stage.

Thompson's presentation of her initial foray into show business is similar. According to her statements to the American press during her first tour, Thompson was a genteel young woman who turned to the stage to support her mother. Her poor, artisan-class father died when she was very young; her mother's remarriage to a prosperous Quaker businessman enabled Thompson to receive dancing and singing lessons. When her stepfather died, Thompson put her skills to work. Here Thompson's narrative begins to follow a separate course than Cushman's. Thompson claimed that audiences were captivated by her early performances. In her first public performance, as Little Silver Hair in a Christmas pageant, her childhood beauty stole the show from more seasoned performers; she continued to impress audiences with her talent and her good looks.[15] Although Thompson couched her initial decision to embark on a stage career within a narrative of familial sacrifice, she suggested that her talent and beauty so entranced her audiences that she was simply compelled to continue.[16] Thompson's explanation of her theatrical career focused on her unsurpassed beauty and popularity rather than on sacrifice, morality, and denial.

Thus, she continually promoted herself as a beautiful and desirable young woman. Before her New York debut she, her husband and manager Alexander Henderson, and publicist Archie Gordon sent press releases to all the major New York papers focusing on Thompson's reputation as a heartbreaking beauty: "At Cologne, the students insisted on sending the horses about their business and drawing the carriage that contained the object of their devotions themselves. . . . Captain Rudolf Baumbarten of the Russian dragoons, took some flowers and a glove belonging to Miss Thompson, placed them on his breast; then shot himself through the heart, leaving on his table a note stating that his love for her brought on the fatal act."[17]

This advance publicity, although criticized as vain hyperbole by some members of the press corps, did influence how audiences and critics viewed Thompson and her troupe. Reviewers usually noted the physical beauty of troupe members before critiquing their performance. Reviewing the premiere of *Ixion,* on October 1, 1868, the *Spirit of the Times* called Thompson "not the least bit of an actress" who was "happy in the possession of a magnificent figure and a pretty face." Further, Thompson was "an energetic, self-confident young lady, who knew she possessed attractions and meant to show them off to the best advantage."[18] Throughout Thompson's long career in burlesque entertainment she used advance publicity to guide reviewers to her physical attributes rather than to her theatrical talent.

Charlotte Cushman, on the other hand, presented herself as celibate and chaste, focusing critical attention on her technical virtuosity in morally pure roles and productions. In many ways Cushman's spinster status contradicted conventional domestic ideology; however, she continued to enjoy both financial success and public approval despite her iconoclastic choices. Among the most notable of these was her decision not to marry. In an age that seemed to prize marriage for women above all else Cushman framed this choice in moral terms. Biographer Lisa Merrill suggests that Cushman was acutely aware of the accusations of whorishness that dogged all performing women and that she explained her decision to surround herself with intellectual female companions and to forgo marriage as a result of her natural distaste for the baser elements of domestic relations.[19] In her published writings, letters to friends, and diaries Cushman described men as unscrupulous predators, seeking to control a woman's body and soul. Among her friends and family she referred to marriage as prostitution and publicly complained that many women settled for marriage rather than struggling to forge careers of their own.[20] Thus, Cushman framed her spinsterhood as a personal choice in line with her own natural chastity. Of course, biographers and theatre historians now tend to read a different narrative.

Cushman's wide circles of female friends and intense, long-term relationships with writer Matilda Hays and sculptor Emma Stebbins suggest to many that Cushman was a lesbian, whether or not her relationships with other women included physical, sexual contact. Seen in this light, Cushman's ability to frame her celibacy within the precepts of the Cult of True Womanhood is even more remarkable.

For some historians Cushman's lesbian identity explains in part her success in breeches roles.[21] Denise A. Walen argues that "Cushman's sexuality is related to her desire and ability for cross-gender performance. . . . The theater afforded Cushman a space in which she . . . could become a desiring subject."[22] Thus, Cushman's breeches performances might now be understood as the theatrical performance of lesbian sexuality. However important this theoretical understanding of Cushman's sexuality may be to current theatre studies and lesbian and gay histories, it is also important to note that during Cushman's lifetime her performances were read very differently by the majority of her public. Cushman's portrayal of the Shakespearean heroes Romeo, Hamlet, and Cardinal Wolsey, as well as her other breeches roles, were hailed as technical masterpieces. Cushman was particularly famous for her ability to erase her femininity in service to her art, and she used the breeches role to enhance her reputation as a theatrical genius.

In London during the 1845–46 season Cushman played Romeo to her sister Susan's Juliet, cementing both their reputations.[23] Cushman seems to have successfully disguised her gender during this and other performances. The *Illustrated London News* averred that "we have never seen the character better played. In her burst of anger or despair we altogether lost sight of the woman: every feminine characteristic was entirely thrown aside in her powerful interpretation of the *role*."[24] Throughout her long career Cushman continued to play Romeo; after Meg Merrilies it was her most popular and most frequent role. Even in her fifties, when she had grown, in the words of her mother, "as fat as a great porpoise,"[25] Cushman continued to persuade audiences she was an adolescent, romantic, male lover. Cushman, never noted for her physical attractiveness, seems to have been particularly adept at male roles and did not use them to advertise a (hetero)sexual availability.

Cushman's success in male roles stemmed precisely from a disjuncture, real or constructed, between her physical body and her characters, nascent lesbian desire notwithstanding. In one version of her critical biography the sight of the stately, sober Cushman in breeches simply could not titillate audiences as did legitimate actresses such as Fanny Kemble and Sarah Bernhardt. Rather, without the distraction of an attractive pair of legs, audiences focused on Cushman's voice, physical characterizations, and presence. Whether or not Cushman was unattractive, this narrative conforms to the broader deprofanation and professionalization of the actress's body in which Cushman's performances participated. She practiced her technique throughout her career, rehearsing even familiar signature roles continually in an effort to refine her intellectual and emotional connections with her characters. Cushman also stressed the physical signifiers of masculinity. Her early opera training and later coaching by William Macready had developed her naturally low voice as a powerful signifier of masculinity. At 5 feet, 6 inches she was taller than most Victorian women (and many men). Her powerful body, strong jaw, and brooding eyes also lent themselves to male characters. Critics noted Cushman's physical suitability for masculine roles: "for intensely feminine as are some of the characteristics of her acting, she has a masculine vigor of style and masculine power of voice that render it possible for her, in a great degree, to sink the woman in assuming the male role."[26] Further, Cushman selected heroes from the Shakespearean canon, a choice that ensured her performances would be read as participating in the most technically demanding, moral, and intellectual theatrical sites. Thus, by stressing the intellectual and physical labor required to play Shakespearean roles, Cushman focused attention on her technical skill rather than on her body.

Not so Lydia Thompson. The cross-dressed woman on the illegitimate stage of the burlesque show, ballet theatre, and music hall appeared not to highlight her acting skills but her physical features. What theatre critic and actress Olive Logan contemptuously labeled "the leg drama" traded on female physical display in order to increase audience appeal. For burlesque performers cross-dressing signaled immorality and sexual availability. These gender-bending performances were viewed as particularly threatening, as the burlesquers' sexuality was highlighted rather than subsumed by playing male roles. Lydia Thompson's gender-ambivalent roles on stage—neither fully female, as with Restoration and eighteenth-century actresses, nor fully male, as with Cushman—were seen to threaten masculine and feminine roles offstage in Victorian society.

In the specific example of burlesque the cross-dressed female entertainer may have been particularly threatening because burlesque had a long history as a *male* entertainment, using travesty for much of its humor and appeal.[27] The shift from all-male to all-female casts suggests that some of the hysteria greeting Thompson and her troupe was related to women usurping traditional male roles and genres. In the post–Civil

War United States, burlesque shows included songs and dances, stereotypes played for comic effect, topical humor, parodies of politicians and
political speech making, and walk-arounds, where each performer pa-
raded in front of the audience displaying his or her particular talent
for applause.[28] In the case of Thompsonian burlesque greater significance was attached to the walk-around, in which audiences responded
primarily to the performer's physical appearance rather than to his or
her theatrical accomplishments. These performances were sometimes
self-reflexive and ironic, calling attention to the shock of the cross-
dressed woman to mitigate her threat. The final image presented to the
audience, however, was the cross-dressed woman talking back to the
spectators.

Thompsonian burlesque combined the traditional elements of parody,
song-and-dance routines, topical humor, and the walk-around with the
spectacle of scantily clad women. The British Blondes and their imita-
tors appeared onstage tightly corseted into low-cut bodices that left
their arms bare. They also wore short pants, knickers, or short, loose
skirts with flesh-colored stockings.[29] Although not particularly scandalous to present-day audiences, female burlesque performers displayed a
great deal of skin and wore clothes that drew attention to their legs,
bust, and hips at a time when hoop skirts to the floor constituted conventional attire. Some Victorian Americans railed against the spectacle
of "nude" women onstage; Olive Logan complained that burlesque performers presented the "disgraceful spectacle of padded legs jiggling and
wiggling in the insensate follies and indecencies of the hour."[30] Needless
to say, the overt display of female sexuality challenged more conserva-
tive feminine ideals.

In addition to appearing in a relative state of undress, female burlesque performers included songs, dances, and innuendo designed to
highlight their sexuality. For example, *Ixion, or the Man at the Wheel*
told the story of a mortal man, Ixion, who seduced several Greek god-
desses. Audiences saw Lydia Thompson as Ixion dressed as a "man" in
corset and short pants flirt with and ultimately seduce Blondes Pauline
Markham (Venus) and Alice Logan (Juno). The burlesque was peppered
with references to wedding nights, soft kisses, and creamy flesh; the cast
sang popular songs such as "While Strolling in the Park One Day,"
which told the story of a chance romantic encounter in the park, and
performed the cancan, jigs, hornpipes, and the ubiquitous walk-around.
Exposing hip, bosom, and leg, as well as a healthy interest in sexual
activity, the Blondes presented a new image of femininity to theatre

audiences, one that upset traditional expectations of burlesque performances, women onstage, and female sexual behavior.

A close reading of the actresses' publicity photos clarifies distinctions between cross-dressed actresses on the legitimate and illegitimate stage. In one of her famous studio portraits Thompson stands on a rocky path in a flimsy, light-colored tunic, light tights, and high-heeled black leather boots. The tunic stops midthigh and is tightly cinched at the waist, leaving her neck, arms, shoulders and a good deal of her chest bare, as well as exposing most of her legs. Her wavy blonde hair is encircled with a garland and flows down her back. Thompson stands with one arm at her side and the other at her waist, legs shoulder-width apart, and her head turned at a three-quarter profile. Although the photograph is labeled "Lydia Thompson as Ixion," she seems more to be posing for the camera than playing a theatrical role. The sartorial elements—high-heeled boots, her own blonde hair, the tight waist, and exposed bosom—foreground Thompson's femininity, although the male name and quasi-Greek masculine attire suggest Thompson's masculine identity.

The photograph of Charlotte Cushman as Romeo, on the other hand, taken late in her career, disguises her gender. Cushman's loose tunic is dark, heavy velvet with long sleeves, high neck, and a skirt that reaches her knees. Cushman wears flat shoes, a floppy hat, and a short wig. A metal belt slung low about her hips holds both a sword at her side and what appears to be a dagger at her crotch, suggestions of phallic power too obvious to ignore. Her legs are crossed, obscuring their shape, and one hand rests at her hip as she leans against a balcony. Although Cushman too is clearly posing for the camera, the "period" hat, flat shoes, heavy tunic, and sword, as well as the pensive expression on her face, mark her as an explicitly theatrical character in a way that Thompson's portrait does not.

The contrast between these two photographs demonstrates the different conventions of breeches roles in legitimate and illegitimate theatre. The public believed that Cushman donned male attire in service to her art, whereas Thompson's costume served the public appetite for sexual display and Thompson's appetite for financial gain. That Cushman was so regarded suggests how fully she was able to frame her performances within the Cult of True Womanhood, something the female burlesquers were both unable and perhaps unwilling to do. Further, Cushman's performances were taken as "true" impersonations of masculinity, perhaps unsurprising given her audience and venue. On the illegitimate burlesque stage, audiences enjoyed Thompson's gender blurring to the alarm of some middle-class critics. Examining the actresses' careers, public personas, and their negotiation of the Cult of True Womanhood reveals how representations of femininity and female sexuality informed hierarchies between high and low theatre in mid-Victorian America.

Notes

1. William Dean Howells, "The New Taste in Theatricals," *Atlantic Monthly,* May 1869, 642.

2. The Cult of True Womanhood's precepts should not be understood to have dictated the lives of all women; middle-class women, as well as their lower- and upper-class counterparts, negotiated many of its rules for behavior. However, the Cult of True Womanhood *was* a determining discourse for much of Victorian America and so warrants consideration here. For a further discussion of female sexuality and the Cult of True Womanhood see Martha Vicinus, ed., *Suffer and Be Still: Women in the Victorian Age* (Bloomington: Indiana University Press, 1973); Carroll Smith-Rosenberg, *Disorderly Conduct: Visions of Gender in Victorian America* (New York: Oxford University Press, 1985); Mary Poovey, *Uneven Developments: The Ideological Work of Gender in Mid-Victorian England* (Chicago: University of Chicago Press, 1988); and Lucy Bland, *Banishing the Beast: Sexuality and the Early Feminists* (New York: New Press, 1995).

3. Smith-Rosenberg, *Disorderly Conduct,* 110–12.

4. For example, *Godey's Lady's Book,* the bible of middle-class Victorian women, ran articles about emancipation and temperance, short stories about women forced to work to support their families, and travel dispatches from London and Paris alongside recipes, fashion news, and sentimental poetry and prose glorifying women's role as moral center for family and country.

5. Lawrence Levine, *Highbrow/Lowbrow: The Emergence of Cultural Hierarchy in America* (Cambridge: Harvard University Press, 1988), 63–69. Levine, following academic tradition, uses the New York City Astor Place Riots as a turning point in the hierarchizing of culture. See also Robert C. Allen, *Horrible Prettiness: Burlesque and American Culture* (Chapel Hill: University of North Carolina Press, 1991), 58–77.

6. Theatre histories tend to frame the actor as an artist struggling for respect and recognition. For many historians the success of actors such as David Garrick, Sarah Siddons, and William Macklin, who seemed to combine technical virtuosity with moral refinement and bourgeois respectability, marks the shift in the estimation of theatre professionals. For more specifics see Jonas Barish, *The Anti-Theatrical Prejudice* (Berkeley: University of California Press, 1981); Oscar C. Brockett, *History of the Theatre,* 5th ed. (Boston: Allyn and

Bacon, 1987); and Joseph R. Roach, *The Player's Passion: Studies in the Science of Acting* (Ann Arbor: University of Michigan Press, 1993).

7. For more on the position of Victorian actresses see Tracy C. Davis, *Actresses as Working Women: Their Social Identity in Victorian Culture* (London: Routledge, 1991). Davis's research, although conducted only in Great Britain and focusing primarily on the years 1870 to 1890, provides a basis for claims about how all Victorian actresses may have been viewed.

8. Denise A. Walen, " 'Such a Romeo as We Had Never Ventured to Hope For': Charlotte Cushman," in *Passing Performances: Queer Readings of Leading Players in American Theater History*, ed. Robert A. Schanke and Kim Marra (Ann Arbor: University of Michigan Press, 1998), 42.

9. For biographies of Cushman see Henry Augustin Clapp, *Reminiscences of a Dramatic Critic with an Essay on the Art of Henry Irving* (1902; reprint, Freeport: Books for Libraries Press, 1972); Doris Faber, *Love and Rivalry: Three Exceptional Pairs of Sisters* (New York: Viking, 1983); Joseph Leach, *Bright Particular Star: The Life and Times of Charlotte Cushman* (New Haven, Conn.: Yale University Press, 1970); Lisa Merrill, *When Romeo Was a Woman: Charlotte Cushman and Her Circle of Female Spectators* (Ann Arbor: University of Michigan Press, 1999); Emma Stebbins, *Charlotte Cushman: Her Letters and Memories of Her Life* (1879; reprint, New York: Benjamin Blom, 1972); and William Winter, *The Wallet of Time* (New York: Moffat, Yard, 1913).

10. "The British Blondes" is a bit of a misnomer. The troupe was officially called the Lydia Thompson Troupe in advertisements and press notices during their first season in the United States. In about February 1869 newspapers such as the *Spirit of the Times* and the *New York Times* began referring to the troupe as "the Blondes" or the "British Blondes," presumably to highlight their physical features and émigré status. Historians tend to refer to the troupe as the British Blondes, and I have continued this practice here.

11. For biographies of Thompson see Allen, *Horrible Prettiness;* Bernard Sobel, *Burleycue: A Pictorial History of Burlesque* (New York: Putnam, 1956); William C. Young, *Famous Actors and Actresses on the American Stage*, vol. 2 (New York: R. R. Bowker, 1975); and Irving Zeidman, *The American Burlesque Show* (New York: Hawthorn Books, 1967).

12. I do not mean to overstate burlesque's importance as a cultural phenomenon; the rhetoric surrounding the Blondes and similar troupes was limited mainly to New York City, and the backlash lasted only a few months. Further, Thompson herself seems to have perpetuated the controversy as much as any newspaper editor or moral crusader. However, to relegate burlesque to the status of a cultural "safety valve" (thus discounting its potential for social commentary and reflection) seems to elide the role burlesque and female burlesque played in representing existing Victorian tensions regarding class, gender, race, and immigration.

13. Merrill, *When Romeo Was a Woman*, 23.

14. Ibid., 18. Merrill and others have established that Cushman exaggerated her family's genteel roots and purposely left out portions of her biography, especially regarding her parents' marriage and her grandmother's life story in order to present a solidly middle-class front.

15. Young, *Famous Actors,* 2:1076.

16. Thompson regularly made recourse to this excuse. For example, on June, 8, 1869, at the height of antiburlesque hysteria, Thompson wrote to the *New York Times,* suggesting that she hoped for the "continuance of kindly support and approval" critics had previously lavished on the British Blondes. If audiences enjoyed her burlesques, how could critics withhold their praise?

17. Quoted in Allen, *Horrible Prettiness,* 7.

18. Review of *Ixion, New York Times,* Oct. 1, 1868, 6.

19. Merrill, *When Romeo Was a Woman,* 252.

20. Ibid., 169.

21. The breeches role traditionally signaled that performing women displayed their bodies and personalities for male approbation. During the nineteenth century, however, the conventions of the breeches role underwent a significant shift. Legitimate actresses increasingly took on male roles, especially from the Shakespearean canon, to prove that their technical skill was on par with their male counterparts. Female burlesque performers, on the other hand, appeared cross-dressed for sensational effect, continuing a spectacular performance tradition rooted in the early English public stage. For more on traditional breeches roles see Pat Rogers, "Breeches Roles," in *Sexuality in Eighteenth-Century Britain,* ed. Paul Gabriel Bouce (Manchester: Oxford University Press, 1982).

22. Walen, " 'Such a Romeo,' " 43.

23. Cushman did not play any breeches roles during her first London season, even though her Romeo was immensely popular in the United States prior to her tour. She explained to friends and managers that she wanted British audiences to see her in highbrow feminine roles; for this reason she also eschewed playing Nancy Sykes and put off Meg Merrilies. Further, she explained her choice of Romeo as a favor to her sister; Susan, newly widowed, needed a strong performer with whom to work in order to achieve any theatrical success (see Merrill, *When Romeo Was a Woman,* 81–83).

24. "Haymarket Theatre," *Illustrated London News,* Jan. 3, 1846, 19.

25. Quoted in Merrill, *When Romeo Was a Woman,* 221.

26. Quoted in ibid., 134.

27. For more on the early American burlesque see David Dressler, "Burlesque as a Cultural Phenomenon" (Ph.D. diss., New York University, 1937), 18–25; and Allen, *Horrible Prettiness.*

28. Burlesque adopted many of the conventions of minstrelsy, including singing and dancing, parody, topical humor, and cross-dressing. Marjorie Garber notes that female impersonation in minstrel shows was divided into two types: the low, comic "Funny Old Gal" and the romantic "wench." These male-

to-female transvestite figures were double cross-dressers: men playing women, white playing black. Following from Garber, the transvestite figure of the minstrel show troped tensions about the increasingly blurred racial and gender categories of post–Civil War America. For more on the specifics of minstrelsy see Eric Lott, *Love and Theft: Blackface Minstrelsy and the American Working Class* (New York: Oxford University Press, 1993).

29. Young, *Famous Actors,* 2:1075.

30. Olive Logan, *Before the Footlights and Behind the Scenes* (Philadelphia: Parmelee, 1870), 586.

Cross-Dressing in Nineteenth-Century Frontier Drama

Roger Hall

IN "TENNESSEE'S PARTNER" Bret Harte described the frontier as a place where people were christened anew. What he meant, of course, was that individuals adopted new identities and started life fresh. They took advantage of the archetypal "second chance" that the opportunities on the frontier provided. In David Belasco's 1905 classic *The Girl of the Golden West,* Minnie, the heroine who runs the local bar, echoes Harte when she observes that all the miners in the little town of Cloudy Mountain, California, go by invented names, having previously discarded some other reality.

Disguise, or the assumption of a new identity, is a hallmark of drama, whether it be the comedic antics of mistaken identity or the more serious concerns of intentional deception. Melodrama in particular frequently employs the device of disguise to advance the plot, and the relative isolation of frontier outposts enhances the plausibility of such traditional dramatic devices.

Cross-dressing—females dressing as males or males as females—is often a subset of the disguise device. Just as disguise or assumed identity gained plausibility from the remote frontier settings, so, too, the disguise of women as men gained plausibility in an environment where most of the population were males. As a result there are numerous instances in nineteenth-century plays set on the American frontier in which women disguise themselves as men and labor in traditionally masculine occupations such as soldiers, miners, or couriers.

Laurence Senelick writes that females often assume male clothing "to flee a man" and "always to benefit from male privilege such as rights of . . . safe travel."[1] That certainly is the case in plays set on the American frontier, for in those plot-driven dramas a woman dressed as a man for one of two reasons: either to escape villainous pursuers or to operate more effectively in a predominately male world while pursuing a love interest. In every instance in which a female donned male clothing, she eventually returned to female garb, admitting her true sex and affirming the status quo.

In one instance, however, an actress wrote a play for herself in which she starred as a powerful male character. This play created a distinctive gender-bending landscape, and its uniqueness was accentuated by the fact that the author and star performer billed herself as "the only American Indian actress."

The use of breeches roles by actresses as a means of "sexual display" or as a "showcase for feminine pulchritude" has long been a standard ploy in theatrical presentation.[2] However, based on available visual evidence, that does not seem to have been a significant factor in the cross-dressing that occurred in frontier plays.

The earliest example of cross-dressing in a frontier play occurs in Mordecai M. Noah's *She Would Be a Soldier; or, The Plains of Chippewa*, which opened at New York's Anthony Street Theatre in June 1819 and used the western front of the War of 1812 as a backdrop.[3] In this play Noah creates a sharpshooting and sharp-tongued female in a breeches role who pursues her lover within a frontier setting. Christine, the daughter of Jasper, a Frenchman who fought with Lafayette in the Revolutionary War and then settled near the Great Lakes, rebels when her father insists she marry a wealthy local boor. Christine disguises herself as a male and follows her true love, Lieutenant Lennox, to the front. Christine misinterprets Lennox's attentions to the general's daughter and, distraught, enlists in the army after proving her shooting skill.[4] When the jealous Christine tries to break into the general's tent, she is imprisoned and sentenced to death. In the end, however, Lennox leads the Americans to victory and rescues Christine. In the character of Christine, Noah devised a courageous, well-educated, and forthright woman, skilled in the frontier arts, who also exhibits a romantic streak. Her adoption of men's clothing, her skill with a rifle, and her defiance of convention to pursue her own desires established a model that was frequently copied by later authors of frontier women.

A second instance of a woman disguising herself as a man in order to pursue a man she loves occurs in Harry Meredith's *Ranch 10*, which played Haverly's Fourteenth Street Theatre in New York in August 1882 and emerged as the first significant play set on a cattle ranch. Also known by its subtitle, *Annie from Massachusetts,* the popular piece used old theatrical devices, which included having an actor play dual roles and putting a character in disguise. Act I is set outside Aunt Coriander

Lucretia Smalley's Ranch 10 ranch house.[5] Annie of the subtitle is Annie Smalley, who is visiting her aunt to recuperate from lung problems. After Annie announces her engagement to Al McClelland, a cowboy at the ranch, Al writes to his twin brother, Tom, a miner in Colorado, inviting him to the wedding. Tom arrives just in time to be mistaken for Al and is arrested for the murder of Silver Bud, a native maiden who worked at the ranch and was infatuated with Al. As Al searches for the real killer, Annie learns Tom's real identity and falls in love with him. At this point Annie decides to find Al and tell him that her affections have changed. She dresses as a man to make traveling easier and sets out after Al, only to find him severely injured in Tom's Rocky Mountain cabin, where he dies in her arms. Eventually Annie returns and proves that Silver Bud was killed by her jealous suitor, Joseph "Red Bullet" Kebook. That revelation prompts Joe's arrest, and Annie and Tom are united at the final curtain. Whereas Christine in *She Would Be a Soldier* was already a healthy woman and an excellent shot, for the frail Annie the adoption of men's clothing becomes a declaration of her independence and an outward manifestation of her new-found strength and courage.

More common than cross-dressing to pursue a lover, however, was cross-dressing to escape the clutches of a villain. One play in which a female character adopts male disguise to elude a villain is *The Limited Mail*, by Elmer Vance, first acted in New York in October 1890 and performed for several years on tour.[6] *The Limited Mail* was one of numerous plays written after the completion of the transcontinental railroad in 1869 that featured the train as a prominent element within the frontier landscape. This "comedy drama" sets the action at a small way station of the Union Pacific railway in Redwood, Arizona, where Nellie Harland lives with Zeke and Nancy, who adopted Nellie as an infant. Nellie loves Charlie Morton, the conductor of the Limited Mail, who travels to San Francisco to care for his wealthy, bedridden uncle. While he's away, John Giddings courts Nellie, whom he knows to be Morton's uncle's secret daughter and heir. Feeling trapped, Nellie dons men's clothes and takes a telegraph operator's job at lonely Floodwood Cut, where she spoils Giddings's plans to rob the train. Her heroism reunites her with Charlie, the conductor of the train, and leads them to unravel Giddings's evil actions and solve the mystery of Nellie's birth.

A more widely known instance of a female disguising herself to escape villainous pursuit occurs in *The Danites; or, The Heart of the Sierras,* which first appeared in New York in August 1877. The play starred the husband-wife team of McKee Rankin and Kitty Blanchard and was based on Joaquin Miller's *First Fam'lies in the Sierras*. In Miller's story a good woman arrives at a mining camp and transforms the environment. Two mining partners vie for her affections until one wins out. Eventually, she bears a child in a scene reminiscent of Harte's "The Luck of Roaring Camp."

In the dramatic adaptation of Miller's story a tale of Mormon revenge was added to the frontier romance. Suspicion surrounded the Mormons from the moment Joseph Smith founded his church in 1830, and it followed them to their sanctuary in the Great Salt Lake Valley. During years of oppression the Mormons allegedly established a secret group to wreak vengeance on their persecutors. This group, called by various names including the Danites, reportedly sought revenge on the killers of Joseph Smith and on their descendants.

The play sprang from the gruesome story of a man named Williams, who participated in the jailhouse raid that led to Smith's death. Soon after that event Williams, his wife, three sons, and, finally, his daughter, Nancy, died under mysterious circumstances, all, it was alleged, victims of the Danites. The inclusion of the Mormon violence turned out to be extremely timely, for in September 1877, just a month after *The Danites* opened, the government indicted Orin Porter Rockwell in Provo, Utah, for murders committed in 1858. In that incident, known as the Aiken massacre, Mormons killed six men they suspected of spying. Although the Aiken episode was entirely separate from the Danites' revenge, advertising copy for the play referred to both stories. In addition, the name Bill Hickman, one of the Danites in the play, comes from one of the men implicated in the Aiken murders.[7] Here, as in other frontier plays, the authors blended various border names and incidents to provide an exciting mixture with a patina of authenticity.

The Danites focuses on a young woman, Nancy Williams, who disguises herself as prospector Billie Piper to elude the Danites, who have butchered her family.[8] She takes refuge in a mining camp in the Sierra Nevadas, at the center of which is "The Howling Wilderness" saloon, peopled with sundry mining types such as Charlie Godfrey, who boasts the ironic moniker of "Parson" because he can outswear any man in the camp, and Alexander "Sandy" McGee, a former wagon master, played by Rankin. Into this mix the author throws "The Widder," Huldah Brown, who arrives to educate the miners. Sandy and the parson both court Huldah, who eventually declares her love for Sandy. Meanwhile, a pair of secretive Danites stalk Nancy.

At Sandy's cabin a year after he and Huldah marry, the encroaching influences of society are visible as the newly domesticated miners celebrate the first child born in the Sierras. The genial atmosphere dissipates, however, when the parson, unable to live happily near the woman he loved so dearly, leaves the camp, and the jealous Sandy orders Billie to stay away from his wife. In the final act the parson returns from his self-imposed exile to prevent the miners, urged on by the disguised Danites, from attacking Billie. After the two Danites are recognized and summarily lynched, Nancy Williams steps out of her disguise, freed at last from the vengeance of the Danites.

The Danites' pursuit of the defenseless young woman gave the play an emotional conflict and a powerful focus. The terrifying pursuit of a young girl by agents of a mysterious conspiracy not only lent itself to melodramatic construction but also touched a raw sexual nerve, for the public viewed the Mormon practice of polygamy as a dangerous threat to proper moral values. Not surprisingly, the government outlawed the practice just five years after *The Danites* opened.

Photographs of Kitty Blanchard disguised as Billie Piper are worth examination. They show her with a pickax and pan, and within the context of the play Billie works alongside the other miners. The photograph is interesting for another reason as well. Cross-dressing in the theatre has long been associated with sexual titillation because women in pants reveal more of their form than women surrounded by layers of petticoats and dresses. The photograph of Kitty Blanchard as Billie Piper, however, shows a woman in dark, baggy clothes, with her curly hair pulled up under her hat. The disguise works in a surprisingly realistic way. There is little overtly womanly about the miner in the photograph.

Although overt sexual allure seems absent in the cross-dressing in *The Danites,* sexual confusion arising from Nancy's disguise most certainly played a vital part. As Sandy and the parson compete for Huldah's affection, both become jealous of her attentions to the apparently male Billie. Huldah has discovered Billie's real identity and agreed to keep it a secret, but their intimate conversations, hugs, and physical closeness infuriate Sandy and the parson.

In the four plays I have mentioned, female characters disguised themselves as men for one reason or another, but there were other instances of cross-dressing in frontier plays. Occasionally an actress simply played a male role, as popular eastside New York star Fanny Herring did in February 1874, when she undertook the role of Uncas in a stage adaptation of James Fenimore Cooper's *The Last of the Mohicans.*

Far more intriguing, however, is the case of Gowongo Mohawk, who billed herself as "the only American Indian actress." She also wrote the play that became her starring vehicle, *Wep-ton-no-mah, The Indian Mail*

Carrier.[9] For at least twenty years Mohawk toured her play throughout the United States and Great Britain, and every time she set foot on the stage she challenged boundaries of ethnicity and sexuality. Although she challenged some boundaries, however, she conformed to others.

Gowongo Mohawk was born on the Cattaraugus Reservation near Gowanda in western New York, a descendant of the Senecan chief Red Jacket. Her father, Ga-na-gua, an elder of the tribe, sent his daughter to a seminary school in Painesville, Ohio. There, she said, she developed an interest in drama and a powerful individualistic streak. She began acting in the late 1880s, just after she completed her schooling. She married Charlie Charles while she was performing with the Michael Strogoff company, and together they wrote a play in which she could star.[10]

The plot of *The Indian Mail Carrier* is rather conventional, and the setting of the play illustrates one of the ways Mohawk conformed to the tenor of her times, for despite the fact that she was an eastern Indian, she located the action on a western ranch. Colonel Stockton owns the ranch, and there the brave Wep-ton-no-mah saves his daughter, Nellie, from a stampede. That incident demonstrates one of Mohawk's unconventional choices, for she played the heroic male role. When Nellie rejects the advances of evil Spanish Joe and speaks admiringly of Wep-ton-no-mah, the infuriated Joe tries to shoot Wep-ton-no-mah but unwittingly kills his father instead. Wep-ton-no-mah signs on as a mail carrier at the nearby fort, thinking he can use his freedom to travel to track down his father's murderer. After several near misses Wep-ton-no-mah finally corrals Spanish Joe and defeats him in a vigorous knife fight.

Although the plot was stereotypical, Mohawk staked out less-conventional territory in several ways. The opening scene immediately signified one difference between Mohawk's play and a typical western melodrama. As they assist with the roundup, the natives in this play enjoy an amicable relationship with whites and are clearly an integral part of the frontier society. The economic interplay between the whites and the tribe is even more vividly presented in the second act at Ga-na-gua's camp, where Spanish Joe bargains for ponies.

Yet another way in which Mohawk's production was peculiar was in her own limited time onstage, especially for a featured actress. The title character hardly appears in the first act. At one point Wep-ton-no-mah rides past on his horse, but even his rescue of Nellie from the stampede is narrated rather than shown. Reviews of Mohawk's performance may explain her restricted stage time. Although reviewers credited her with "a truly magnificent contralto voice," one critic commented that she speaks with "a singularly pronounced and idiomatic" accent, and another wrote that she "reads her lines in a sort of monotonous chant."[11]

By producing her own material Mohawk made a declaration about her status as a woman in a dramatic world of heroic males, as a Native American in a white society, and as a Native American within the specifically white, European theatrical tradition. She acted, she said, because she loved the stage—a prime reason for a performer of any background. She also wanted to protest wrongs done to Indians and the manner in which Indians were portrayed on the stage. She stated, "People used to want me to dance—to play the banjo and do fancy steps. I said, 'No—that is no fit thing for an Indian.' It is beneath his dignity—dancing like a common street player. I saw an Indian dancing in variety once, and it was a shameful sight. . . . He looked so out of his element. I said, 'Look at that. Is that pretty or natural?' Ah! It was ugly and pitiful."[12]

A third reason for her work was her desire "above all things to prove that the Indian is capable of the highest civilization." In other words she used the European paradigm of theatre to validate Native American worthiness. Other Indians, she claimed, "are very proud indeed of me, and look upon me as a person whose business it has become to show the white people that the Indian is not a savage."[13] During this late-nineteenth-century period politicians and social reformers hotly debated the assimilation of Native Americans, and the educated Gowongo Mohawk, making her living in the European theatrical tradition, certainly stood as a living exemplum of successful assimilation.

Many plays—*The Danites* and *Ranch 10* are two examples—disguised female characters as males. A female performer actually playing a male role, however, was more unusual. In this case, especially because of stereotypes of native maidens, Mohawk's decision to play a male role is as striking as her determination to star onstage as a Native American actress. From the reality of Pocahontas to the dramatic invention of Edwin Milton Royle's *The Squaw Man* the stereotype for the native maiden was to befriend and love a white male. Rather than conform to that stereotype Mohawk cast herself in the position of the heroic male. One reason may have been her physical appearance. She was described as "very tall" and "wonderfully muscular," and one review relates how she "flings a stalwart ruffian over her shoulder as though he were an orange."[14] A more potent reason for her choice of roles may have derived from her own active personality. She liked to ride and rope and to shoot guns and arrows. She decided to enact a male role, she said, because she wanted to do something "wild and free" and thought playing a male role would allow her greater opportunity for riding and wrestling.[15]

Although Mohawk played the role of the heroic male avenging the death of his father, the play avoids the conventional pairing of hero and heroine. Perhaps the fact that she was a female playing a male led her to avoid a traditional ending because it would have meant coupling two actual females, although such unions were not unheard of on the American stage. Or perhaps, despite Mohawk's actual history of marrying a white, she was reluctant to pair a Native American with a white partner in her play.

Although she enacted a hard-riding, knife-fighting male in the play, Mohawk emphasized more traditionally female attributes in interviews. Writers described her as "graceful" and commented that she made all her own clothes and costumes. She wore European-style clothing that nevertheless reflected her heritage: a blue serge dress was trimmed with brass balls, and another gown was decorated with beadwork.[16]

The images in a publicity collotype, however, provide a different perspective, sending striking and obviously calculated messages. The actress sits with legs crossed wearing fringed leggings appropriate to her male character and suggestive of her native background. She holds a riding crop in her left hand, and a large western-style hat hangs on her knee. An American flag draped on a table beside her declares her patriotism, and handguns, spurs, holsters, and bullets lie prominently on the flag, silently proclaiming both her physical skills and the action-oriented material in her plays. She signed her photos "Aboriginally Yours, Gowongo Mohawk."

Mohawk played a male hero in at least one other play, *The Flaming Arrow*, by Lincoln J. Carter. *The Indian Mail Carrier*, however, remained Mohawk's staple vehicle. In 1893 she took the play to England, where, like many American frontier melodramas, it received positive responses during a two-year swing through London, Liverpool, and other cities. She toured the play as late as 1910.

All of the plays I have mentioned to this point involve a female character disguising herself as a male or a female performer enacting a male role. In only one play before movies took over the frontier genre does a male character disguise himself as a female, and that occurs in Walter Woods's melodrama *Billy the Kid*, which first played New York at the Star Theatre in August 1906.[17] In the play the young Billy the Kid becomes an outlaw and pursues the villainous Boyd Denvers, who killed Billy's mother and stepfather. At one point in the action Billy's girlfriend, Nellie, helps him escape Denvers's henchmen by dressing him as a woman. Eventually Denvers, who is revealed to be Billy's father, is accidentally killed by his own men, and Billy conveniently adopts a new identity and marries Nellie.

The male-to-female cross-dressing in *Billy the Kid* is distinctly different from the female-to-male variety in other frontier plays. Billy is disguised as a female for only a few moments, whereas the females are disguised as males for major sections of the plays. Although he dons a dress to escape his pursuers, Billy performs no traditionally female activities, unlike his female counterparts, who, disguised as men, undertake a variety of male activities. Finally, although Billy's disguised escape occurs at a climactic moment in the play, it carries with it a humorous edge, rather like Huck Finn dressing up in Mark Twain's novel, that is unlike any of the disguised female adventures.

In the plays set on the frontier, disguise reinforced the image of the West as a place of new identities and fresh starts but also as a place of potential danger. When a woman switched to a man's garb—as Nancy Williams did in *The Danites* or as Annie Smalley did in *Ranch 10*—she also assumed a masculine self-sufficiency. There is no one else to take care of Nancy when she transforms herself into Billie Piper. The frail Annie from Massachusetts, by donning a man's ranch clothing, physically reconfigures herself as a strong and independent western individual who actively pursues her desires. In the end, however, both women gladly emerge from their disguises and return to their culturally approved female roles.

The case of Gowongo Mohawk, on the other hand, despite the fact that she wrote and starred in a conventional melodrama, presents a far more unusual case, for her career onstage represented a singular achievement for her as a woman and as a Native American.[18]

Notes

1. Laurence Senelick, *The Changing Room: Sex, Drag, and Theatre* (London: Routledge, 2000), 159–78; the quotation appears on 162.

2. Ibid., 211, 270.

3. *She Would Be a Soldier* is in Richard Moody, ed., *Dramas from the American Theatre, 1762–1909* (Cleveland: World Publishing, 1966).

4. That Christine violates powerful social and religious prohibitions by taking on the uniform of a soldier (see Senelick, *Changing Room*, 165) seems not to be a factor in the play.

5. Harry Meredith, *Ranch 10; or, Annie from Massachusetts* (Chicago: Howard and Doyle, 1882).

6. A typed manuscript of *The Limited Mail,* by Elmer E. Vance, copyrighted in 1889, is in the Rare Book and Manuscript Collection at the Library of Congress.

7. An undated advertising paper in *The Danites* file, Billy Rose Theatre Collection, New York Public Library for the Performing Arts, relates the stories.

8. Although the overall scheme is similar, Joaquin Miller's published version of the play, *The Danites in the Sierras,* differs in some aspects from the version acted by McKee Rankin, based on reviews of the production. For an examination of those differences see Roger Hall, *Performing the American Frontier, 1870–1906* (Cambridge: Cambridge University Press, 2001), 92–103. Joaquin Miller's *The Danites in the Sierras* is in Allan Gates Halline, ed., *American Plays* (New York: American Book Company, 1935; reprint, New York: AMS Press, 1976).

9. A typed manuscript of *Wep-ton-no-mah, The Indian Mail Carrier,* by Gowongo Mohawk and Charlie Charles, copyrighted in 1892, is in the Rare Book and Manuscript Collection of the Library of Congress.

10. Biographical information is from the *Era* (London), May 20, 1893; and from Alice W. Byre, "From Wigwam to Stage," an unidentified article in envelope 1495, Locke Collection, Billy Rose Theatre Collection, New York Public Library for the Performing Arts.

11. "An Indian Actress in England," *Era* (London), May 20, 1893; and *Des Moines Register and Leader,* March 28, 1910.

12. *Des Moines Register and Leader,* March 31, 1910.

13. Quotations in this and the previous paragraph are from "Indian Actress in England"; and *Des Moines Register and Leader,* March 31, 1910.

14. *Vanity Fair,* Feb. 1, 1901; Eyre, "From Wigwam to Stage"; and "Indian Actress in England."

15. *Des Moines Register and Leader,* March 31, 1910.

16. Ibid.; *Vanity Fair,* Feb. 1, 1901; *Era* (London), April 15, 1893; and Eyre, "From Wigwam to Stage."

17. *Billy the Kid* is in Barrett Clark, ed., *America's Lost Plays,* vol. 8 (Princeton, N.J.: Princeton University Press, 1940; reprint, Bloomington: Indiana University press, 1965).

18. For more on the subject of how the frontier was presented on American stages before movies see Hall, *Performing the American Frontier.*

Clean and Sober

Women Celebrity Endorsers and the 1883 Pears' Soap Campaign

Sherry J. Caldwell

I N TODAY'S MEDIA-DRIVEN CULTURE Americans are bombarded with celebrity endorsements touting the advantages of credit cards, fine jewelers, communications networks, athletic shoes, and snack products. Some celebrities are as well known for their commercials and public service announcements as they are for their creative and athletic accomplishments. Celebrity endorsement is big moneymaking business and valuable exposure for both celebrity and advertiser. According to Alexander Walker stars "are the direct or indirect reflection of the needs, desires and dreams of American society."[1]

Writers of advertising history generally consider the 1920s to be the time when film "stars" began to dominate the press and the new "modern" advertising. But performers took their place in the media and advertising long before the widespread popularity of film and the development of modern advertising techniques. Theatrical personalities have served as models for the American public for well over a century. Advertisements for products carrying celebrity names and endorsements became a major feature of the American advertising landscape in the 1880s, beginning in earnest with the appearance of a landmark advertising campaign by A. and F. Pears', Ltd., in 1883.

From its expansion and development in 1862, Pears' Soap, under the leadership of Thomas J. Barrett, had employed the resources of the press for advertising and publicity. Prominent skin specialists, doctors, and chemists provided testimonials that appeared in magazine and newspaper advertisements, on handbills, and on posters.[2] But in 1883 Pears' initiated a groundbreaking campaign that would alter the face of advertising and the status of theatrical celebrities, particularly women, into the present time. In a series of advertisements that filled entire pages of national newspapers and magazines in England and America, Pears' Soap displayed the endorsements of three of the world's most beautiful women: performers Mary Anderson, Lillie Langtry, and Adelina Patti.[3]

Benjamin McArthur, in *Actors and American Culture, 1880–1920,* demonstrates the rising social status of the legitimate actor in the last decades of the nineteenth century through cultural changes linked to urbanization, lessening resistance from the church, and professionalization. By the late nineteenth century, performers "dwarfed the roles they played" and had become the significant element in entertainment for a public that craved human images. One of the central factors for this change was the burgeoning magazine industry and the resulting influence of the media. "[A]ctors had become celebrities in their own right, embodying images of personality and lifestyle that the public found immensely attractive. A new relationship between actor and society had been formed, aided by revolutionary changes in the field of journalism."[4]

One such change was the vast expansion of national publications. These highly illustrated magazines of the 1880s carried commentary on the drama, articles on the offstage life of performers, and features of theatrical life, some contributed by the celebrities themselves. The American public had an insatiable curiosity for every type of news concerning their favorite players. For players who had long recognized the value of publicity the new mass-distributed magazines provided vastly expanded opportunities for national press coverage at the time when touring combination companies were experiencing their heyday. Although performers made their reputations from road campaigns and booked tours in New York, fortunes were made "on the road." Nationally distributed and sold at reasonable rates (the dime magazine emerged during this period), these new magazines provided coverage that contributed greatly to a performer's national recognition and stimulated interest (even if for scandalous reasons), which translated into box-office dollars.

The explosion of advertising that accompanied this publishing phenomenon coincided with the advent of theatrical celebrities in a variety of product advertisements that appeared alongside theatrical articles and features. Manufacturers advertised products named for the famous: Maxine Elliott cosmetics, Lillian Russell hats, and Julia Marlowe shoes. Theatrical celebrities, especially actresses, endorsed products from soap and corsets to pianos and patent medicines. As early as the 1860s, collectible photographs of famous personalities were advertised in magazines such as *Godey's Lady's Book*. Considerable financial gain could result from endorsements, either directly as compensation or indirectly at the box office, as a result of the recognition gained through the widespread exposure these advertisements provided.

Advertising in the modern sense was just beginning to emerge in the years following the Civil War. A number of factors combined to set the stage for its expansion: urbanization; expansion of railroads; growth of manufacturing; national distribution of product; technological advancements in papermaking, printing, and photography; favorable governmental postal regulations; lowered restrictions by publishers for size and style of ads; vast growth in national magazines; and institutionalization of advertising.[5] Although newspapers were plentiful and widely read, they generally carried advertisements for local purveyors; national magazines, however, carried advertisements for manufacturers intended to raise consumer consciousness, particularly for brand names. Nationally distributed magazines provided the publicity required by performers to build and maintain a national audience. By the 1880s the illustrated display advertisement, influenced by the French poster, became the trend. And from early on advertisers directed their messages to the middle-class female consumer.

The endorsement advertisement—the testimonial—was one method advertisers used to reach their audience.[6] According to Robert Atwan, following the Civil War, "as printed salesmanship evolved into modern advertising, pictures of the highly born, the powerful, and the celebrated became a permanent feature of America's system of selling."[7] "Celebrities of all types—opera singers, prize fighters, movie stars, baseball players, explorers—were all available at the right price. The celebrity became a new kind of folk hero. It was he whom middle-class Americans now wished to emulate rather than the aristocrats of Park Avenue and Newport, who had formerly been America's tastemakers."[8] Atwan accurately places the prevalence of celebrity endorsements by performers to the last decades of the century when the "great stars of theater and opera—Sarah Bernhardt, Enrico Caruso, Lillian Russell, the idols of America's rapidly growing urban middle-class—often offered an endorsement of some product."[9] How-tos of advertising indicated the importance of matching endorser to product. How better to put across Pears' simple message—"that Pears' Soap was safe and healthy and that it made its users beautiful"[10]—than to showcase beautiful celebrity women?

Leonard de Vries has observed that "part of the function of advertisers has always been to sell dreams and the dream they induce with the greatest success is the dream of beauty."[11] The three women chosen by Pears' had two things in common. They were very well known, and they were considered extremely beautiful. Despite (or perhaps because of) numerous public scandals, they were chosen by Pears' to represent its product, suggesting acceptability to its targeted consumers—upper- and middle-class women. This emphasis on appearance as an overriding condition for selection was unprecedented and reflected the growing focus on physical attractiveness in American culture.

It is curious that theatrical women should emerge as endorsers of commercial products at this particular time. In her study of soap advertising in Britain between 1875 and 1914 Kelley Graham demonstrates ways in which advertisers "pay great attention to what the society already believes, and how an extension of truncation of those beliefs can be commercially exploited."[12] Society generally believed, as it had for centuries, that theatrical persons, particularly women, were sexually and morally suspect despite any argument that status of performers was on the rise. The national press delved into personal lives and thrived on scandal, yet it continued to disparage divergent behavior. Public image, which now reached well into offstage lives, played a central role in the nature of a performer's celebrity. Advertisers sought the most appropriate match of product to endorser to audience. Pears' was a luxury product marketed to the upper middle class and above. The right endorser needed to reflect those values held by Pears' customers and by the Pears' company—celebrities with a "clean" public image. An examination of Pears' celebrity endorsers, however, including the influential minister Henry Ward Beecher, reveals contradictions between such an ideal match and a celebrity's public image, illuminating a new phenomenon regarding the position of performers in media culture in the last decades of the nineteenth century and in the sociocultural fabric of America.

Photography had completely revolutionized pictorial reproduction in the 1870s and 1880s. Like the painted portrait, the photograph could provide a greater intimacy with the subject through close-ups. Unlike the painted portrait, the photograph could be inexpensively mass produced, making that intimacy widely accessible. Images of prominent persons were sold in expensively produced and bound collections and in the inexpensive *carte de visite* and cabinet-sized photograph. "It is not possible to measure the impact of photography unless we accept the carte de visite for what it was—the most popular ad diversified type of photography produced in the nineteenth century."[13] Sold in theater lobbies and shops, in collections from publishers and directly from photographers, these photographs satisfied the demand created by "cartomania," the absolute craze for collecting photos. One way advertisers capitalized on this fad for collecting photographs of the famous was to insert images of celebrities as part of the endorsement. This strategy was used to great advantage by Pears' Soap in the presentation of the endorsements of Anderson, Langtry, and Patti.

Although some actresses had attained a position of respect with an admiring public for their talents, accomplishments, and moral lifestyles, the historical prejudice against women in the theatre had certainly not yet dissipated. This prejudice was founded on a number of conditions inherent in theatrical life: the public nature of performance threatened modesty; close proximity to men created familiarity, jealousy, and temptation; and continuous traveling prevented women from occupying their proper place in the home. Additionally, women in the theatre often assumed the role of breadwinner, a role prescribed to men, and in doing so compounded prejudices against them. For these reasons (and more) women in the theatre held a questionable public image, even in the last decades of the nineteenth century, when the Cult of Personality and the Cult of True Womanhood met head-on. The position of actresses in relation to women in other fields is characterized by Lois Banner in *Women in America:* "In exceptional fields like the theater, well-known prima donnas like Lillian Russell and Lily Langtry commanded huge salaries for their appearances, while newspapers wildly gave them publicity. . . . There was still an aura of disrespectability about the actress, but the profession offered some mobility for women, and the actress was beginning to assume the role of cultural model that by the 1930s she would so powerfully play."[14]

Beyond the generalized, historical prejudice, certain factors had a direct effect on public image, one of which was marital status; multiple marriages or divorces had a predictably negative consequence. Another was a choice of roles. Shakespeare and other classics were considered respectable. Works that could "influence [the public] for good" were preferable to those that "drag one through the mire of immorality even when it shows a good lesson in the end."[15] A third factor, of greatest concern here, was the growing emphasis on physical attractiveness, increasingly evident as the "leg business" began to gain ground with the popularization of burlesque. Olive Logan criticized this focus on appearance because it demoralized the theatre and provided employment for the untrained and untalented.[16] Although she and others continued to speak out against this type of spectacle, as Faye Dudden demonstrates, the objectification and commodification of the female body only became more prevalent. Moreover, "the tendency to exalt appearances over ability . . . also witnessed the increasing importance of physical appearance in American society at large."[17]

Pears' Soap was a leader in its field and a leader in advertising, spending between thirty thousand and forty thousand pounds per annum in the 1880s.[18] Despite the questionable reputations of women in theatrical professions, Pears' chose to present three highly recognizable performers, women noted for their beauty, to represent their fine soap to upper- and middle-class female customers. The exemplary lives that would have reflected the ideal virtues of the class of women to whom the advertisements were directed were sorely lacking in all but one of the 1883 Pears' endorsers.

It is important to note certain features about the series of 1883 ads before examining the public images of the celebrities. Each endorser probably appeared in more than one version (design) of the advertisement. It is feasible that the ads may also have been distributed in handbills because Pears' made such distributions habitually. In addition to ads displaying individual endorsers, Pears' released ads that displayed all three endorsements, including that of a fourth endorser, Henry Ward Beecher, the influential American religious leader. Beecher, in his written endorsement, equates cleanliness, and Pears' Soap in particular, with godliness. The advertisement first appeared on the whole of the front page of the *New York Herald*.[19] By combining the endorsement of Beecher with the three actresses, Pears' may have attempted to head off resistance to the actresses and give them additional legitimization. One of the most interesting of the combination advertisements, which appeared in *Youth's Companion* in 1889, shows Beecher in the center with four beauties surrounding him, their faces in flowering pears. Below the images Beecher's testimony appears, and under that the caption reads, "Brains and Beauty. The Church and the Stage Unite in Praise of 'Pears' Soap.' For the Face and Hands." Pears' also produced full-sized (eight-by-ten-inch) photographic portraits on plaques, available for five cents in postage stamps. Issued three years after the campaign first began, the ad's text was printed on the reverse side so that the portraits would be suitable for display. Each of the photographs is a simple, classical portrait in profile. The only woman wearing jewelry is Patti, but even she is wearing only a collar pin and earrings. Langtry is wearing her

Advertisement for Pears' soap. *Youth's Companion,* 1889

hair in the well-known knot at the nape of her neck. The women appear demure and passive. Positioning the actresses in profile may have made retouching the silhouettes easier, the retouching an attempt to bring particular facial features in line with popular standards of beauty and to neutralize ethnic features during a time of increasing anxiety over immigration. (Beecher is not in full profile.)

At the time the Pears' ads appeared Mary Anderson was a star of the American stage, Adelina Patti was a celebrated diva of the opera world, and Lillie Langtry was a distinguished member of London's cult of highborn "Professional Beauties."

What were professional images? Anderson was highly respected. In her short eight years on the stage she had attained a secure position among America's finest performers. On the brink of her first London appearance in the fall on 1883 she wrote, "The chief good my work had accomplished . . . was the assurance . . . from many young men and women that the examples of such characters as Parthenia, Ion and Evadne . . . had helped them in their daily lives and strengthened them in moments of despondency and temptation." At the age of fourteen she first realized that acting was a "serious art that might be used for high ends," and she dedicated her professional career to trying to perfect that art. In two of her most famous roles, Parthenia and Galatea, she wore Grecian robes, and the Pears' ads show her dressed in the same manner.[20]

Patti was at the top of her profession and had been since her New York debut in 1859. According to the *London Illustrated Sporting and Dramatic News* she "leaped with one bound, from comparative insignificance, to the highest pinnacle of popularity."[21] Her success was built on perseverance and self-discipline. Celebrated in Russia, France, Italy, Spain, and Austria, she returned to tour the United States in 1882 for the first time in twenty-three years.

Langtry had made her entrance into London society in 1876 but because of a series of changing circumstances found herself in need of an earned income, so she turned to the stage. After a short London engagement in a small role, in the summer of 1882 she traveled through the British provinces and arrived in New York for an expansive tour of the United States in the fall. Early reviews of her work were kind, but audiences went to see Langtry as much out of curiosity as for any expectation of good acting.

With which roles were these performers connected? Patti performed in opera, still the territory of the elite and royals. An accomplished musician, she performed a wide range of roles in Italian, English, and German; no one questioned the high quality of these works. Anderson's repertoire included many of Shakespeare's heroines, and because of her own aversion to anything but good characters in good plays, the moral tone of the plays and roles she attempted was of the highest order. Langtry had only been performing for a year by 1883, so her repertoire was quite limited. Thus, at the time the ads appeared, it was too early in her theatrical career to judge her public image through the roles she chose to perform.

If marital status was indeed a measure of one's image, both Patti and Langtry fell far short of the virtue admired by upright middle-class women. Patti was first married in 1868 to the querry to Napoleon III, but in 1876 she fell in love with a notorious, womanizing tenor, Ernest Nicolini. Amid storms of scandal she was granted a legal separation from her husband in August of 1877. According to the *New York Times* of March 9, 1877, Patti's "running away with a common tenor, after being for so many years a titled and respected lady, held up as a model to all young ladies upon the stage, was almost beyond conception."[22] Although her divorce was not granted until July of 1885, during her 1882 U.S. tour she performed and lived openly with Nicolini.

Langtry's story was even more scandalous. Shortly after her arrival in London society she began an affair with the Prince of Wales, later King Edward VII. Although she was a married woman at the time, they conducted their affair openly (within the prescribed social circle). Langtry's familiarity with the prince was common, as she knew he would be dressed as Pierrot at a costume ball where she appeared as Pierette. During the party she put ice down his back, displaying physical contact, which further insinuated the intimacy her costume had suggested and constituted highly inappropriate behavior.[23] Shortly thereafter, she discovered she was pregnant and went into hiding until her daughter was born. Although London society and the public were unaware of her child, her position as mistress to the prince and the social acceptance it entailed had ended, so she embarked on her stage career.

Anderson is the only one of the three to have escaped moral scandal. She traveled with her mother and her stepfather and, with the exception of appearing on the stage, maintained the standards of her strict Christian upbringing. Whereas both Langtry and Patti actively sought publicity, wearing extravagant jewels and expensive gowns, traveling in luxurious private railroad cars, marrying several times, and generally defying convention, Anderson was quite the opposite and found the public side of celebrity its most disconcerting aspect.

At first glance the earlier observation that Beecher's appearance in the Pears' Soap campaign may have mitigated resistance to the women seems reasonable. However, in 1875 Beecher became embroiled in "the greatest sex scandal of the century," involving the wife of a parishioner/business partner, which resulted in a highly publicized trial.[24] Despite confessions by all involved, the influential Council of Plymouth Church exonerated him, and the jury could not agree on his guilt; nonetheless, the scandal was front-page news for years, and the American public had devoured every word.

Mary Anderson, Lillie Langtry, and Adelina Patti were considered three of the world's most beautiful women. Patti, as evidenced by reports and photographs, maintained her youthful beauty well into late middle age. When she appeared in concerts, she dazzled audiences with her magnificent gowns and jewels, all of which flattered her five-foot, two-inch figure with its seventeen-inch waist and size-two shoes.[25] Langtry had a very fair, milky-white complexion and initially gained attention by dressing very simply, unadorned by any jewelry, with her hair in a simple twist. This was the look that first attracted Millais, who painted the famous portrait that gained her the title "The Jersey Lily." The public flocked to see her portrait at the Royal Academy and avidly collected her photographs. She set trends with her hairstyles and her fashions, and "at the age of twenty-seven, having accomplished nothing whatever in her life, she was the heroine of millions."[26] Throughout her career she made an annual pilgrimage to the House of Worth to purchase an extensive wardrobe, a practice she shared with Patti. "The acknowledged beauty queen of the stage . . . was Mary Anderson. The soft, regular features of her face suggested to some the reincarnation of a Greek goddess and she possessed an air of purity and refinement, an incorruptible innocence that caused the public to take her into their hearts as 'Our Mary.' "[27] Anderson took pains to approximate historical and regional accuracy in her stage costumes but was not known for wearing high fashion or for being a style setter.

Historical information about the details of these ads is sparse and contradictory. The only biographical studies to have recounted the participation of the three women in the Pears' campaign are those written about Lillie Langtry, and each tells a different story. Pierre Sichel credits Henriette Hodson (Langtry's mentor and manager in her bid for the stage) for initially suggesting the endorsement. Noel Gerson seems to credit Langtry with the decision to appear for Pears': "Shortly before the news was announced that Lillie intended to invade the United States, another storm broke. Lillie created a new precedent by being the first woman to endorse a commercial product. . . . Ladies of quality were horrified, and it was said in high circles that Mrs. Langtry sold herself with the abandon of a prostitute. It would be more than [a] decade before impoverished aristocrats followed The Jersey Lily's example and began to endorse commercial products."[28] James Brough hints that the connection between the Prince of Wales and Pears' (Pears' held the royal warrant) may have influenced Lillie's appearance. Although they do not agree about how the ad came about, all three biographers note the negative reaction of Langtry's social circle.

What circumstances might have prompted these women to appear in an endorsement at a time when theatre folk were making concentrated efforts to become more socially acceptable and when appearance in the ads would have threatened that social position? Neither Patti nor Anderson needed the financial gain, and Langtry's fee of 132 pounds, if typical, was not a windfall.[29] Although both Patti and Langtry challenged convention, Anderson was too protective of her personal privacy and too dedicated to her "art" to have ventured into product endorsement on her own. The inducement(s) to participate must have been powerful to get all three to offer their endorsements.

At the time of the Pears' campaign each performer was planning a landmark engagement: Anderson was to appear in London for the first time, Langtry was about to launch an extensive first tour of the United States, and Patti was planning her return to the United States after an absence of more than twenty-three years. Further, all three were working under the management of Henry E. Abbey, who had managed the wildly successful publicity-ridden U.S. tour of Sarah Bernhardt in 1880. The Bernhardt tour was widely recognized for the enormous amount of merchandising—"manufacturers cashed in with Sarah Bernhardt perfume, candy, cigars, and eyeglasses"[30]—and for the vast amount of publicity it generated, some through events executed expressly for press attention. Abbey was a man who "wielded great power within the theatre."[31] Although biographies and memoirs of the four women (including Bernhardt) do not go far in characterizing Abbey's role in developing publicity schemes for their tours, it seems possible that he was instrumental in engineering this rather unusual campaign, which lasted for at least six years.[32]

The longevity of the campaign and the known variations of advertisements that appeared suggest a successful result for Pears'. Although it is not possible to gauge the full impact for the actresses, each of their engagements was a critical and financial success. The Pears' campaign may also have increased the longevity of their careers; with the exception of Mary Anderson, who retired from the stage in 1888, their sources of income continued into the twentieth century. All three endorsed other products—corsets, throat lozenges, cosmetics, pianos, patent medicines—indicating they must have been encouraged by the experience of appearing in the Pears' campaign. In succeeding years many women of the entertainment world would follow in their footsteps, including Viola Allen, Emma Calve, Beatrice Cameron, Fanny Davenport, Maxine Elliott, Virginia Harned, Anna Held, Mary Mannering, Nellie Melba, Lola Montez, and Olga Nethersole.

The 1883 Pears' Soap advertising campaign broke established conventions of testimonial advertising by presenting the endorsements of three women of the theatre. The campaign was also innovative in its scope and longevity. More important, by prioritizing the factor of beauty in the selection of three women, it mirrored society's (and the theatre's) growing emphasis on appearance, increased the social status of performers, and helped promote the theatrical celebrity's position as model for the middle-class consumer. Celebrities and advertisers that followed Pears' lead created a trend that remains an ongoing part of American culture.

Notes

1. Alexander Walker, *Stardom: The Hollywood Phenomenon* (New York: Stein and Day, 1970), 13.

2. Tim Shackleton, introduction to *Bubbles: Early Advertising Art from A. and F. Pears Ltd.,* ed. Mike Dempsey (London: Fontana Books, 1978), 3.

3. The 1883 campaign also featured Henry Ward Beecher. Later ads included the testimonials of Miss Fortescue, Marie Roze, and/or Sarah Bernhardt. As had been the case with the initial campaign, these later endorsements appeared singly or in various combinations.

4. Benjamin McArthur, *Actors and American Culture, 1890–1920* (Philadelphia: Temple University Press, 1984), 142.

5. The importance of professionalization for the acting profession illustrated by McArthur was just as crucial to establishing respect for advertisers, a rather renegade occupation prior to the 1870s.

6. Invoking the names of the prominent was an age-old strategy for the promotion of products and services. Prior to the nineteenth century the aristocracy served this purpose; later new methods of production and changing attitudes to health and science brought the "scientific expert" to the fore. Considered a proven advertising strategy, testimonials are mentioned in advertising histories, instruction manuals, and in-house organs. William M. Freeman notes,

e.g., that "[t]he core of the testimonial in advertising is the endorsement of the product or the idea by an individual. It represents identification of the prospect with the satisfied user. When the prospect, who may not know he is one, sees a well-known personality (rich, famous, handsome, respected, admired, successful or with any desirable characteristic at all) using the product and happy with it, a favorable reception is created for the product or idea" (William M. Freeman, *The Big Name* [New York: Printer's Ink Books, 1957], 35).

7. Robert Atwan, *Edsels, Luckies, and Frigidaires: Advertising the American Way* (New York: Dell, 1979), 283.

8. Victor Margolin, Ira Brichta, and Vivian Brichta, *The Promise and the Product: Two Hundred Years of American Advertising Posters* (New York: Macmillan, 1979), 73–74.

9. Atwan, *Edsels,* 283.

10. Shackleton, *Bubbles,* 5.

11. Leonard de Vries, comp., *Victorian Advertisements.* Text by James Laver (London: John Murray, 1968), 40.

12. Kelley Graham, "Advertising in Britain, 1875–1914: Soap Advertising and the Socialization of Cleanliness" (Ph.D. diss., Temple University, 1993), 127.

13. William C. Darrah, *Cartes de Visite in Nineteenth Century Photography* (Gettysburg: W. C. Darrah, 1981), 13.

14. Lois W. Banner, *Women in Modern America: A Brief History* (New York: Harcourt Brace, 1974), 6, 8.

15. Mary Anderson, *A Few Memories* (New York: Harper and Bros., 1895), 15.

16. Olive Logan, "The Nude Woman Question," *Packards Monthly,* July 1869, 193–98.

17. McArthur, *Actors,* 41.

18. Lori Ann Loeb, *Consuming Angels: Advertising and Victorian Women* (New York: Oxford University Press, 1994), 9.

19. Shackleton, *Bubbles,* 3.

20. Anderson, *A Few Memories,* 127, 129.

21. John Frederick Cone, *Adelina Patti: Queen of Hearts* (Portland, Ore.: Amadeus Press, 1993), 80.

22. Ibid., 117.

23. Carmelina Marie Raines, "Lillie Langtry: The Construction of Self through Spectacle" (master's thesis, University of Wyoming, 1996).

24. Banner, *Women in Modern America,* 118.

25. Cone, *Adelina Patti,* 80.

26. Kelley A. Gerson, *Because I Loved Him: The Life and Loves of Lillie Langtry* (New York: William Morrow, 1971), 74.

27. McArthur, *Actors,* 42.

28. Gerson, *Because I Loved Him,* 89–90.

29. James Brough, *The Prince and the Lily* (New York: Coward, McCann, and Georghegan, 1975), 276; Gerson, *Because I Loved Him,* 89.

30. McArthur, *Actors,* 37–38.

31. Ibid., 19.

32. The question of brokerage is one for further inquiry. At a time when the ranks of theatrical producers and managers began to be filled by men from the world of business rather than the theatre, contracts between managers and performers began to take on a new weight.

Post-Symposium Discussion

An Excerpt

Susan Stockbridge Cole, Elizabeth Reitz Mullenix, Lisa Merrill

ERM [ELIZABETH REITZ MULLENIX]: This morning, Lisa [Merrill] and Susan [Cole] and I talked about themes that we felt had emerged at the conference. And so what we'd like to do is list off those themes for us all to consider, make some comments about those, and then have a dialogue with you. We thought about six different themes, the first being the idea that women are caught between two worlds in the nineteenth century, that they must work within an exploitive or oppressive system in order to progress. And then we also thought about agency, which could also be talked about in terms of resistance or in terms of transgression. The third theme we saw was some sort of containment strategy, some sort of way to assuage or mitigate some kind of threat that particularly female proponents forwarded. The fourth theme was the idea of gendering the space, and the fifth idea was the discussion of gender with the absence of race and class and sexuality as well. And then the sixth theme was the commodity relationships and spectacle. Those were the six things that we thought about and will comment on.

SC [SUSAN COLE]: I was struck, in particular, by a series of paradoxes triggered, in part, by my comments on the Cult of True Womanhood but also [by] the kinds of things that emerged as the papers were given. In the early nineteenth century there was a given set of prescriptions about what [women] had to do in order to be true women and how they worked within that system and gained power. . . . By using the restrictions, particular things, such as doing good works, under the acknowledgment that it was okay to read and to write, and although many things were written just for women, there were many other things that were available to them as a result that they could read, not just nice articles and *Godey's Lady's Book*. In this new leisure they were given permission to do some things and one of those, eventually, was to go to the theatre. The paradox existed between women like Fanny Kemble, who acted the role of true womanhood on the stage but didn't live it in her life, and Charlotte Cushman, who was the very model of the chaste woman onstage. By the middle of the century things were beginning to move, and the women were beginning to move out of that box. So I thought there were some interesting differences and paradoxes in all the papers which talked about many actresses. Lotta Crabtree [a paper presented by Jeff Turner] [was] one of them that I noticed, who played a role onstage that was different from a role in life—[such] actresses played the role as a way of playing the game. Women learned awfully early how to play the system. We've probably always known how to play the system and [to] turn it to our advantage, so sometimes I wonder if we really need to say so much about how we've been oppressed because we've managed to work through it and figure out a way to turn that [oppression] to our advantage.

LM [LISA MERRILL]: One of the things that struck me is that this has been such an enjoyable weekend—being in a dialogue with everyone. But one of the things that strikes me with all this work is that we need to constantly keep in mind *who* we are talking about. First of all, we're talking about gender, which is construction of masculinity and construction of femininity as enacted by women and men, both of whom do both. We've had a wonderful window into some of those representations here, [but] there's lots more. I mean I hope you all leave here as energized as I am, thinking about, "Oh, and I see how this fits my next project," because the discussions have been really productive, I think. Constructions of masculinity and femininity, as constructions, have been presented and sometimes interrogated in some interesting ways here. When we talk about women, the easy, the unconscious, assumption of who is included and omitted in that category always makes me nervous—more so as time goes on. So I've really appreciated those papers and those conference questions, as we've had these wonderful talks after each panel, that keep us asking, who are the women who are not, and men who are not, included in these questions? The majority—the numerical majority, poor women, women of color, people whose expressions and understandings of desire don't fit into normative frameworks. Men and women whose understandings of themselves and representations and participation or resistance to those representations are not normative. I think it's productive for us to look at ways in which we use notions of gender that implicate race and class without mentioning it. Much of what we're talking about is the construction of middle-class whiteness and middle-class white femininity on the stage. That is a productive thing to look [at], and naming it allows us to look at race and class and sexuality as constructions as well as looking at gender as a construction. Some papers have done this because their subjects targeted it. Roger Hall's mention of [Gowongo] Mohawk strikes me as an opportunity for us to have seen that image and understand the beginnings of discussion of and participation in that. Lots of us have been engaging in not just a discussion of race but where class touches; this last session, Noreen [Barnes-McLain]'s, reminded us that prostitutes are not a discrete category separate from the other women in the room. What does that say about class and how people's experiences with class get reflected? One of the many rich things that has happened for me this week is to have this range of texts, many of which many of us are familiar [with], being interrogated from a specific vantage point, such as Marcia [Pentz]'s talk about manliness in *Uncle Tom's Cabin* and Karl [Kippola]'s talk about what Forrest did to the presentation of women's resistance to sexual assault. We're all at the vantage point of trying to imagine what happened to the spectators in the room at that time. These questions of agency that Liz started with are obviously not just a matter of the intentionality of a performer, director, or P.R. person as they set this up. That archival material gives us a window into how people said that to themselves, or others, is an interesting claim and I think important and valuable.

ERM: I was especially interested in that idea of agency, too, that was expressed through Susan's talk in that while there were these kinds of restrictions that women had to deal with that were detrimental in some ways, there were also good opportunities for women. Helen [Huff]'s remarks about the benefit also really played into this idea of female agency and female subjectivity and the idea of [the] performer as author. Lisa's point about thinking of the audience as author is also very significant, I think, and that also needs to be kept in mind. We've discussed Cushman, and the breeches performer claiming a subject position [as well as] Marcia Pentz's paper on Stowe's presentation of a female subject reading female agency and the tension between that and the attempt to contain it in Aiken's stage version. I saw what has been a really interesting theme too in terms of the age and gender codes that Dorothy Holland talked about in *Black Crook* and also, as Lisa mentioned, the silencing of women in *Jack Cade,* and also what Brian [Carney] was talking about in terms of Boucicault engineering his dramas to support a new middle-class agenda. These are all containment strategies in a way; they're all ways to support hegemony. One of the comments that I thought was so interesting yesterday was when Dorothy mentioned that hegemony always tries to create a competition or an adversarial relationship among the disenfranchised in order to maintain its power. And I really saw that as being something that might play into what Noreen [Barnes-McLain] was talking about, too, in terms of female managers vigorously trying to keep women of color and lower-class women out of certain parts of the theatre. There's so many wonderful resonances between all of these papers.

SC: Something that's been interesting to me is the exploration of female sexuality. This was at a time when the relationships between men and women were so restricted, and, therefore, if they were presented on-stage, they were somehow licentious and suspect; the actresses were suspect because they were in intimate connection with men in public. The other part of it is that women lived their lives together in very close relationship; female crushes and friendships and closer relationships were considered a part of the way we lived. Society was homosocial for women, but then they would jump right into heterosexual marriages. I was listening to how many of the actresses discussed in these presentations had failed marriages. It seems to me that is also a reflection of the fact that the male/female relationship was almost an unnatural one because there was no preparation for it. And women stayed because they didn't have any choice, except for actresses, who did [have choices] because they could work.

LM: It seems also true that women were caught in this historical moment where they are, on one hand, trying to work professionally and create a new kind of image for women and, on the other hand, [are] living with this discourse of true womanhood and dealing with the ramifications of that. And I think about Marti [LoMonaco]'s paper on how Lulu Glaser participated in her own commodification in a lot of ways; the idea of her ankles being so fetishized was really something that stood out to me. And yet at the same time she recognized that "I am not existing here," [that] this is not a place for women, and that there could be so much more. And also seeming to be so frustrated that she retired from the stage. And I saw that in Rebecca [Jaroff]'s paper about Charlotte Barnes, too, in terms of her performance of *Octavia Bragaldi.*

The female character asks her husband to enact her revenge because she herself can't do it. Because of the condition of the "femme covert" in the nineteenth century, her husband would be blamed for the crime even though she did it herself. So that even in the surreal kind of situation of, "I want to commit this crime and can't be blamed for it," there's a frustration . . . : "I cannot even enact my own revenge in this kind of society."

ERM: One of the things that both of your comments on sexuality and relationships [brings to mind] is the need to always keep reminding ourselves that heterosexuality is a historical construction as much as homosexuality is. Notions of marriage are different in different historical moments. Certainly the legal status that Lisa was talking about, the "femme covert" status, is one manifestation of the fact that companionate marriage is a middle-class phenomenon that is happening at this time. So the sentimental story of the falling-in-love, marital relationship, whether enacted onstage or experienced in the audience, is a very different life than in our experience of this time. And so we can't read a range of options with an assumption of twentieth- or twenty-first-century heterosexuality. The other thing that I'm thinking about in relation to many of the presentations is the notion of the discursive context that the stage and the written text offer as evidence and material for examination. I think a lot of early theatre historians and critics, as have historians in many other disciplines, made a simple assumption that representations . . . are representation[s] of events, actions, experiences, beliefs that have happened and not that they are instruments in a participation of a discursive construction of the very things they represent. So, for example, whether it's a presentation of homoerotic desire on the part of men or women, or the erotic response to children, the range of things we've talked about this weekend is daunting. But all of those things did work in the world. They didn't just, obviously, represent conditions that existed in the society at the time. The work they did, as representations, has a constituent effect on the spectators who participated in their co-construction. So my little pitch is for looking at spectatorship and to do the hard archival work that I know we're all proud of, to try and look, certainly, at our conventional theatre history resources but [to] look beyond those for the source of material evidence that would help us see how that dialectic worked in both directions and not to hold up this script or that review as evidence of what happened and how it was understood. I think we're in a moment where we've gone beyond that, and this conference is a place that we can keep making that leap. This has been a very dialogic conference, more so than many I've participated in and that's the great strength of this.

SC: I don't remember a symposium at which there was so much overlap and so much interchange. There's always been discussion and questions but rarely real exchange and the fact that so many of you have acknowledged each other as you presented the papers and how they tie together. You have presented us with some new ideas and maybe some directions in which to take further research. Of course a symposium is always exciting, [but] this one's been especially gratifying in that way.

LM: As long as we're being surrounded by these Cushman images, I think the question that we're raising about notions of beauty relates to the pictorial evidence. We can look at the construction of that evidence, under what conditions and for what purposes too, but [we] also [need] to look at our own aesthetic responses and how they are based on class. I think the paper about Pears' Soap [is] starting to point us in the direction of looking at "beauty," how arbitrary it is, and what is missing in this construction of women's attractiveness. This brings me back to some of Liz's points in her talk about having to look at those questions, particularly this larger question of the way cross-dressing onstage is read against the bloomer movement and the look at the social and cultural issues that are happening outside of the theatre.

ERM: That comment that you're saying makes me think about constructing gender in terms of my new project about the Civil War; I'm challenged by comments that I've heard this weekend to look at this construction of masculinity and the ways in which stage performance and national events are in a dialectic. In some of [the] work I'm doing on the construction of masculinity in the Civil War I make the claim that the Astor Place Riot is really about construction of gender. The competing notions of gender and nationality are concepts that are absolutely indicated. You can't talk about gender without nationality, without sexuality, without class. They're all aspects of a particular phenomenon.

AUDIENCE: [Question inaudible]

LM: Age is a really interesting variable there and how that gets gendered.

ERM: I think about the caption on the Pears' Soap ad saying that beauty and brains are separate and the separation of the two is necessary. And to come back to beautiful, we also need to ask whose bodies were read as beautiful, to whom, and how that was consciously read.

ERM: I'm really interested in cultural criticism, the construction of these notions by cultural critics, and [in] identifying who makes these claims about the attributions of beauty or attractiveness. I mean there is a lot of grunt work involved, frankly. It takes a lot of time to find those attributions that give us some clues to whether the interests that are being served by presenting for us . . . the bravado democratic ideal. . . . For example, men wore false calves onstage, to replicate ideal forms. It's not just hypothetical when you have pictorial evidence of what that body looked like, and there is archival evidence of how that body is read and how that looked.

SC: But we don't know because we never saw them. We don't have any way of knowing how these figures looked onstage in action. We see that horrible picture of Cushman in middle age as Romeo. She must have transcended that to a certain extent. I know she was never as popular as she was [as] a young woman in that part, but when you look at the eyes in the picture, we can imagine how she must have been able to project onstage and would transcend some of the physical shortcomings.

ERM: Also, it's reflective of questions that theatre historians are now beginning to ask. This is work about historiography of the audience, and . . . the central question of how did people see is so crucial, and I think it's something theatre historians are just really beginning to focus on. I fantasize with my students all the time that I would still be reading that performance in 1845, reading the archival material, to think about the historiography of an audience.

LM: It's one of the tools that I think is so productive to be in dialogue about for those of us working with students, and you want to help encourage development further in these directions as well as in our own work. I look at work in anthropology because the notion of the path as another means of observing another culture is a method that visits the same tools. And I think historical ethnography and ethnohistory are tools that we might employ as disciplinary moves for those of us who didn't have this opportunity when we were studying because it wasn't a discipline available to us. Those of us working with students need to encourage people to look in those directions because these are the same questions that contemporary enthographers don't want to approach. They approach their subjects in an imperialistic colonizing fashion.

ERM: The question that the theatre historians have been asking is maybe an old question—how did the audience see? We heard that with Susan Kattwinkel's paper on women in Vaudeville this weekend. But because of the interdisciplinary nature now of academia, and because we have acquired these new tools throughout ethnographic studies and women's history and criticism, we can answer those questions in new ways. Joe Roach challenges theatre historians [to] employ these new methodologies in order to answer these old questions. It is a larger theme in terms of what's going on in our field.

LM: I just want to add reference to John [Frick]'s point about theatre historiography. What's interesting to me as much as looking at the larger social and historical contexts—those great things we've done in our work prior—is to look at investigations in our discipline. And so theatre historiography also means engaging, respectfully but sometimes the highest form of respect is criticism—but take your work seriously enough to engage it—to look at the work of prior theatre historians who were, as we all are, creatures of their time and have left us these big gaps and holes in their investigations or subjects and to look at their analysis of their time period and to look at what's missing. What I started to do at the end of my research for [*When Romeo Was a Woman: Charlotte Cushman and Her Circle of Female Spectators*] was to look at all the different ways that Cushman has been depicted. Now I have opportunity to do more. Now we have great new tools, and we want to look at where we've been so that we don't have to keep going over the same trends.

Contributors

Sherry Caldwell is in the process of completing her Ph.D. in Theatre and Performance at the University of Pittsburgh.

Brian T. Carney is a Ph.D. candidate at the University of Pittsburgh, with certificates in Film Studies and Cultural Studies. His dissertation examines the narrative landscape in a group of recent historical fantasies. He is currently working as Business Manager at Miller Auditorium at Western Michigan University. He has presented papers at the Southeastern Theatre Conference Theatre Symposium, the Association for Theatre in Higher Education, the American Society for Theatre Research, and other conferences. He holds the B.A. and B.S.E. from the University of Pennsylvania and the M.F.A. from Southern Illinois University at Carbondale. A director, playwright, actor, and actor coach, he is also artistic director for Lavender Productions.

Susan Stockbridge Cole is Professor of Theatre and Chair of the Department of Theatre and Dance at Appalachian State University in North Carolina where she directs and teaches directing. She is a past president of the Southeastern Theatre Conference, North Carolina Theatre Conference, and Alpha Psi Omega national theatre honor society. She has published articles on nineteenth century American actresses in *Notable Women in American Theatre,* published in 1990 by Greenwood Press and *American National Biography* published in 1999 by Oxford University Press as well as a number of articles in theatre journals.

Roger Hall is Professor of Theatre at James Madison University. His research on nineteenth-century American theatre has been published in *Theatre Journal, Journal of American Culture, Theatre Survey, Theatre Studies, Nineteenth Century Theatre Research,* and numerous other publications. His book *Performing the American Frontier, 1870–1906* has just been published by Cambridge University Press. He is also author of *Writing Your First Play,* published by Focal Press and now in its second edition.

Dorothy Holland is Assistant Professor of Theatre at the University of Richmond in Virginia. She received a Bachelor of Science from Skidmore College, an M.F.A. from Sarah Lawrence College, and a Ph.D. in theatre history and theory from the University of Washington in Seattle, where her research focused on the representation of women on the nineteenth-century American stage. Dorothy has written for *Theatre Survey* and was recently awarded a fellowship at the Oberman Center for Advanced Studies at the University of Iowa. She is a member of the American Society for Theatre Research, the Association for Theatre in Higher Education, Actors' Equity Association, the Screen Actors Guild, and the Society of Stage Directors and Choreographers.

Helen Huff is an Assistant Professor in the Speech, Communication, and Theatre Arts Department at the Borough of Manhattan Community College in New York City. She has just finished a year as a visiting professor of theatre at Wake Forest University in Winston-Salem, N.C., where she directed an evening of plays by W. B. Yeats in the WFU Irish Festival. She was awarded her Ph.D. in theatre at the City University of New York in 2000. She has been the online editor of the International Bibliography of Theatre for the past ten years. Her research interests are primarily in the nineteenth century American theatre.

Karl Kippola is a Ph.D. student in theatre at the University of Maryland. His study focuses on the construction of masculinity in antebellum America through the theatricalization of historical events. He presented "In New Dress: Edwin Forrest's Passive Patriotism and Robert T. Conrad's *Jack Cade*" at the American Literature Association (ALA) conference in May 2001 and "Shades of Difference from *The Quadroon* (1856) to *The Octoroon* (1859)" at the Northeast Popular Culture/American Culture Association (NEPCA) in November 2001.

Martha S. LoMonaco is Associate Professor of Visual and Performing Arts and director of the theatre program at Fairfield University in Connecticut. She is an active director and the author of numerous articles, the chapter on Regional Theatre in *The Cambridge History of American Theatre, Vol. 3,* and the book, *Every Week, a Broadway Revue: The Tamiment Playhouse, 1921–1960.*

Lisa Merrill is Professor of Performance Studies, Hofstra University and Visiting Professor of Performance Studies at Northwestern University for 2002. Her most recent book, *When Romeo Was a Woman: Charlotte Cushman and Her Circle of Female Spectators* (University of Michigan Press, 1999) was awarded the Joe Callaway Prize for Best Book in Theatre or Drama. She is currently coediting (with Denise Quirk) a collection of Cushman's letters and working on a new book on nineteenth-century cultural criticism and homoeroticism.

Elizabeth Reitz Mullenix is Associate Professor of Theatre at Illinois State University and is currently acting as interim Associate Dean in the College of Fine Arts. Mullenix has presented numerous conference papers and published articles and book reviews on antebellum culture / theatre, cross-dressing, first-wave feminism, and gender / feminist theory in the *Journal of American Drama and Theatre, Theatre History Studies, Theatre Journal, Theatre Survey,* and *Drama Review.* Her book *Wearing the Breeches: Gender of the Antebellum Stage* was published by St. Martin's Press in 2000. Mullenix served as the Theatre History Focus Group Representative for American Theatre in Higher Education 1999–2001, Conference Planner for the Mid-America Theatre Conference in 2000 and the Theatre History Symposium co-chair in 1999, and has recently been elected to American Society for Theatre Research's executive committee. In addition Mullenix was on the editorial board for Theatre in the Americas, a new performance series published by Southern Illinois Press, and is a consulting editor for *Theatre History Studies.* At Illinois State University Mullenix has also served as both the director of graduate studies and as the director of the masters' program in theatre studies.

Kirsten Pullen received her Ph.D. from the University of Wisconsin-Madison's Theatre and Drama Department. She is currently on the faculty of the Speech Communication Department at Colorado State University.

Laurie Wolf is an Assistant Professor of Theatre at the College of William and Mary, where she teaches theatre history and feminist theatre. She holds a Ph.D. from UCLA and prior to this appointment taught at Goldsmiths College, University of London, where she convened the M.A. degree in Playwriting and Dramaturgy. She has written a critical introduction for Oscar Wilde's *An Ideal Husband* for Nick Hern Books and has coedited a book titled *Performance Analysis: An Introductory Coursebook,* published by Routledge. She is contributor for the *International Bibliography of Theatre,* as well as for *Cassell's Companion to Twentieth Century Theatre* and *Annotated Bibliography of English Studies.* Her current research is on gendered space in nineteenth-century melodrama and women in English Regency theatre.